DESIGNING WITH
Texture

Over 150 ways to

use textures for

scrapbooking,

card making, gifts

and more…

IDEAS BY

Heidi Swapp
Debbie Crouse
Julie Turner
Robin Johnson

WRITTEN BY

Erin Trimble

contents

dedication

Because creativity cannot be scheduled and doesn't happen within "normal business hours," we would like to dedicate this book to our **families**. Your support, encouragement, patience, and love enabled us to create this book. Thank you!

We would also like to acknowledge and thank Allison Tyler-Jones and Donna Smylie. Without knowing it, you brought us together, inspired us, and continually supplied us with fabulous and innovative products to keep our minds creating outside of the box.

welcome

Anything added to a scrapbook page or paper art project contributes to its overall feel, but perhaps the **greatest impact** comes from the surfaces on which you build and from the textures you use. The chapters in this book can be broken down into three categories: soft **surfaces** such as velvet, corduroy, organza, silk, woven fabrics, and printed materials; hard surfaces including glass, plastic, transparencies, chipboard, cardboard, metal, screen, and modeling paste; and **techniques** that can be applied to any surface to expand its range of possibilities, such as crackling, aging, adding acrylic paint or walnut ink, doing rubbings, applying transferred images, and decoupage.

Many of the products we **showcase** have traditionally been used by all types of artists. In these chapters, we will demonstrate how you, a paper artist, can incorporate these products into your projects. As you continue to use and experiment with these products and techniques, you are sure to find that the **possibilities are endless**. Our goal as teachers and artists is to introduce new and innovative concepts which can then be applied to any scrapbook page or paper art project.

We love the **synergy** that can happen between card making, art journaling, and scrapbooking. We hope you will draw **inspiration** for your scrapbook pages from the unique paper crafts, as well as incorporate concepts from scrapbook pages onto your cards and paper art projects. Each chapter is rich with **fresh ideas** and techniques that will stretch your **creativity** and inspire **you as an artist!**

attachments

When your texture won't stick with an adhesive, you can try one of the following "attachments."

Sewing: Hand and machine!

Staples: Look for colored staples at office supply stores.

Brads: They come in many sizes and colors. No tools needed!

Eyelets: You'll need an eyelet setter and hammer to set. They also come in many colors, sizes, and styles.

Snaps: Check out the notions at a fabric store. Many different sizes and colors of snaps are available.

Studs: These are available in many sizes, colors, and shapes.

Pins: These can range from safety pins to straight pins and from embroidery pins to corsage pins.

Clips: Don't forget paper clips (spiral and regular), bulldog clips, alligator clips, and hair clips.

4

Bone Folder

Utility Knife

OLFA

X-Acto Knife

J. Herbin
depuis 1670
Boîte de 12 plumes assorties
Box of 12 assorted nibs

Nibs

Dip pen

ABCDEF
GHIJKL
MNOPQR
STUVWX
YZ&?!;

Crayons

ANCIENT PAGE
ACID FREE ARCHIVAL
WATERPROOF
DYE INKPAD
Coal Black

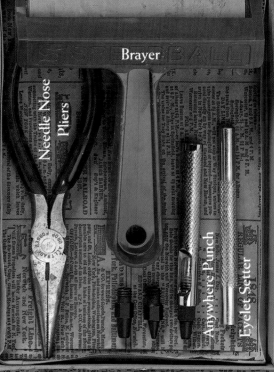

Painter's Comb

Brayer

Needle Nose Pliers

Hole Drill

Hammer

Anywhere Punch

Eyelet Setter

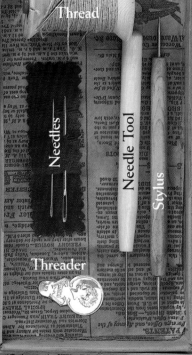

Thread

Needles

Needle Tool

Stylus

Threader

Various Brushes

Sponge

Detail USArtquest, Inc.

8 Americanpainter 4300 SHADER TAKLON SRI LANKA

Sponge Brush

Palette Knife

tools

…and don't forget a snap fastener tool, wire cutters, stapler/staples, tweezers, baby wipes, containers, caddy, and a little imagination!

1 **Glue Dots** (*Glue Dots International*) come in several sizes and varying thicknesses. They are an instant bond, and they work on almost every surface imaginable.

2 **Perfect Paper Adhesive** (*USArtQuest*) is an acid-free adhesive that comes in a matte or glossy finish and is used as a clear sealer for decoupage. It can also be used as an adhesive or mixed with paint or Pearl-Ex to add color.

3 **Spray Mount** (*3M*) is a quick-tack adhesive that can be used to permanently or temporarily bond a variety of surfaces, including paper, fabric, wood, felt, or metal.

4 **Mod Podge** (*Plaid*) is a high-moisture sealant used for decoupage. It dries clear, is available in matte or glossy, and works best when brushed on. (*Comparable to Perfect Paper Adhesive*)

5 **Mono Multi Liquid Glue** (*Tombow*) dries quickly and is great for paper-to-paper adhesions.

6 **Fusible Web** is a great solution for affixing fabric to paper. Follow package instructions, as each brand is a little different. If you'll be using fusible web as an adhesive, then sewing around the edges, be sure to use a lightweight fusible web so your needle doesn't "gum up." And when ironing fusible web to your fabric, place the fabric nap side down on your ironing board as not to ruin the look of the fabric.

7 **Aleene's Tacky Glue** (*Duncan Enterprises*) is comparable to Mono Multi.

8 **PVA** (*Books By Hand*) is a bookbinder's adhesive. It has a high moisture content, so it works best when painted on evenly and smoothed over with a brayer.

9 **Household Masking Tape**, a low-tack tape, can be used to tape off areas on your projects.

10 **Embossing Tape** (*Gary M. Burlin & Co.*) is a super tacky tape that can be used for embossing powder, foils, beads, and glitter.

11 **E-6000** (*Eclectic Products*) is industrial-strength glue for heavy items. It dries clear, so it's ideal for glass.

* **Diamond Glaze** (*JudiKins*) is best described as a dimensional adhesive. The glaze can be layered to make a thick glass-like appearance, or it can be used to adhere glass and plastic.

* **Duo Embellishing Adhesive** (*USArtQuest*) needs to become slightly tacky before placing lightweight embellishments (glitter, sequins, metallic foil flakes, etc.) to it.

* Not Pictured

products

1. Watercolors
2. Liver of Sulfur *(Maid-o'-Metal, St. Louis, Inc.)*
3. Acrylic Paint *(Plaid)*
4. Walnut Ink *(Postmodern Design)*
5. Modeling Paste *(Liquitex)*
6. Image Transfer Pen
7. Inks
8. Embossing Inks & Powders
9. Rub-Ons *(Craf-T Products)*
10. Crackle Medium *(FolkArt)*
11. Pearl-Ex *(Jacquard Products)*
12. Fixative *(Prismacolor)*
13. Etching Paint *(Delta)*
14. Archival Mist *(Preservation Technologies)*

1 velvet&corduroy

When you see a lovely velvet dress or a pair of corduroy jeans, you can almost imagine how they feel without even touching them. Now transfer that sensation to your scrapbook pages and projects. With velvet and corduroy, you instantly add warmth and depth to your creations. Corduroy can even add a touch of masculinity, as seen on Heidi's "Up the Lazy Weber" layout. And velvet can provoke a feeling of elegance or royalty, as Julie illustrates on "The Wedding" page.

A Little Girl
With Big Dreams

I remember Sarah
as a little girl, dramatic
and full of life.
I loved taking pictures
of her whenever I
visited her family.

Today, Sarah is a
confident, young woman
of 26, living out
her dream as an actress
on Broadway. I am
so proud of my niece's
accomplishments.

• • •

August 2002

how to *Stamp Velvet*

Set your iron to medium-high heat. Select a stamp with a bold pattern. Lay the stamp, rubber side up, on the ironing board. Position the velvet, fuzzy (or nap) side down, over the stamp. Carefully press the iron over the fabric for about 15 seconds. You may need to place an ironing cloth between the iron and the fabric to prevent the steam holes from imprinting on the velvet.

To emboss the computer journaling, sprinkle embossing powder over the printed text while it's still wet and heat emboss.

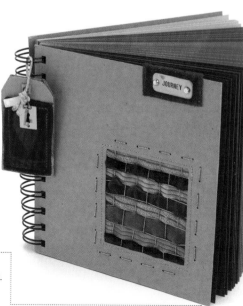

A LITTLE GIRL WITH BIG DREAMS
BY JULIE TURNER

VELVET: Jo-Ann Fabrics
RUBBER STAMP: Inkadinkado
BEADS: Designs by Pamela
BRASS FRAME: Ink It!
EMBOSSING POWDER: Gold Super Fine Detail Powder, Ranger Industries
COMPUTER FONT: Goudy Old Style, WordPro

JOURNEY JOURNAL
BY DEBBIE CROUSE

1/16" HOLE PUNCH: Fiskars
DIE CUT: Accu-Cut
FABRIC: Jo-Ann Fabrics
FUSIBLE WEB: Wonder Under
HEMP CORD AND GOLD THREAD: Darice
BRADS AND EYELETS: Making Memories
KEY AND KEYHOLE CHARM: Ink It!
METAL PLATE: Memory Lane
OTHER: Chipboard

how TO

Cut a front and back cover from chipboard to desired size. Die cut a square out of the front cover. Punch holes around the square, making sure the holes line up on opposite sides. Lace gold thread through the holes, stitching all of the vertical lines. Then stitch all of the horizontal lines. This creates a base for your weaving. Knot the thread on the back. Cut narrow strips of velvet and corduroy about 1" longer than the square. Weave the strips over and under the gold thread. Top stitch around the edge of the square to secure the ends of the fabric. To complete the journal, have cardstock cut to the size of the cover and bind at a copy store. Use an iron-on adhesive for the velvet tab, then stitch over the top. Attach metal plate with brads. Stitch embossed velvet to cardboard tag. Rough up and curl edges of tag.

THE WEDDING

BY JULIE TURNER

VELVET, SATIN, AND FUSIBLE WEB: Jo-Ann Fabrics
BEADS: Westrim Crafts
BUTTON: La Mode
TASSEL: JudiKins
SILK RIBBON: Bucilla
ENVELOPE: Hero Arts
STICKER: Mrs. Grossman's
EMBOSSING INK: Clear Emboss*it*, Ranger Industries
EMBOSSING ENAMEL: Ultra Thick Embossing Enamel, Suze Weinberg
COMPUTER FONT: Tempus Sans, WordPro

how to

Select two contrasting fabrics, such as velvet and satin, and fuse the wrong sides together. Trim the fabric to fit the layout and adhere it to cardstock with spray adhesive. Do not adhere the corner or area that is going to be rolled back. Fold a corner or roll one side to reveal the contrasting fabric. Anchor with a stitch and decorative bead.

For embellishment, lightly sand a sticker to make it look aged and adhere it to an envelope. When embossing the envelope and to ensure you don't seal the opening, slip a long strip of cardstock into the envelope. Dab embossing ink over the front of the envelope, sprinkle with embossing enamel, and heat emboss. Repeat the inking and heat embossing two more times to build up a smooth, glossy surface. Fold the long strip of paper down to cover the already embossed area and emboss the flap in the same manner. The photo mat was embossed using the same layering technique.

TIME CAPSULE

BY HEIDI SWAPP

TAG: American Tag
STUDS: Dritz
WATCH FACE: Manto Fev
COINS: Chuck E. Cheese and Hong Kong
POSTAGE STAMP: England
WOODEN LETTER: Millcreek Designs
PEWTER HEART: Sundance
DOG TAGS: Chronicle Books
SCRABBLE LETTERS: Ink It!
BULLDOG CLIP: Pearl Arts & Crafts
LETTERING: Artist's own handwriting
OTHER: Silk ribbon, velvet, foam core, old book paper, envelope, charms, film negatives, Statue of Liberty button, and jewelry boxes

how to

Cut small jewelry boxes down so the sides are 1/4" tall. Arrange the boxes together and trace the outline on a piece of foam core. Using an X-Acto knife, cut around the outline. Adhere a piece of cardstock to the back of the foam core, then adhere the boxes to the backing (inside the foam core).

To line the boxes, cut paper to fit in the bottoms. Use a spray adhesive to mount velvet onto the paper. This will keep it rigid and clean looking when you line the boxes. Adhere your knick-knacks to the velvet with adhesive dots before adhering the fabric to the boxes.

basic foam core tips:

1. Cut with a straight edge and a sharp X-Acto knife.
2. Do not try to cut all the way through the foam core in one pass of the knife. Plan on making 4 passes with your knife before you get all the way through the foam.
3. Do not glue it all together until the very end and until you are satisfied with how it looks.
4. Trim 1/4" off the width and height of your overall page to insure it will fit in your page protector.

how TO

Cut a piece of corduroy to 12" x 6". Fold one side under to make a finished edge for the pocket. Using a pencil, lightly mark pocket lines on your fabric, large enough for your tags, to help you sew straight lines. Hand or machine stitch the pocket lines. To add extra detail, use different colored thread for each line. After sewing the pocket lines, attach the "passages" title with eyelets. Next, position the fabric on the cardstock and tack it down with a few hidden stitches along the pocket lines. Fold the raw edges back and adhere them to the back of the cardstock. Because the fabric tends to make the page a bit bulkier, you may need to slightly trim your cardstock before beginning.

how to

To create tags with a flap such as "Congrats" or "Get Well Soon," fold a piece of chipboard over about an inch. Place the folded edge of the chipboard just below the top blade of the tag die and cut tag on a die cut machine. Place a swatch of fabric under the flap and machine stitch to hold it in place. Punch a hole near the top edge of the tag and set an eyelet. Embellish tags as desired.

These tags are a great way to use up all of your fabric scraps, even the tiniest piece. Since tags are quick and fun, make several at a time.

PASSAGES
BY JULIE TURNER

CORDUROY AND CANVAS: Hancock Fabrics
EYELETS: Coffee Break Designs
THREAD: DMC
RUBBER STAMPS: Barnes & Noble, Inc. (letters), Inkadinkado (clock)
STAMPING INK: Ranger Industries
TAGS: Sunday International
CHAINS: American Tag
CHARM: Designs by Pamela
WATCH FACE: Manto Fev
COMPUTER FONT: Perpetua, WordPro
OTHER: Pieces of cut sheet protector

NAPPY TAGS
BY DEBBIE CROUSE

TAG DIE CUTS: Ellison and Accu-Cut
FABRIC: Jo-Ann Fabrics
FUSIBLE WEB: Wonder Under
RUBBER STAMPS: Uptown Design (clock), Stampa Rosa (postal cancellation), Hero Arts (French script), Sanford Corporation (C.O.D., 3rd Class Mail, Confirmation), Hampton Art Stamps (floral X), Inkadinkado (Carved in Stone Alphabet), Stamp in the Hand (message line), Eclectic Omnibus (alphabet collage), PSX Design (Antique Alphabet)
STAMPING INK: Black, Memories; Van Dyke Brown, Ranger Industries
TAGS: American Tag
EYELETS: Making Memories
ALPHABET BEADS AND HEMP CORD: Darice
SAFETY PINS AND STRAIGHT PINS: Dritz
OTHER: Chipboard, star pin, button, and wire

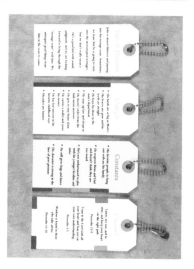

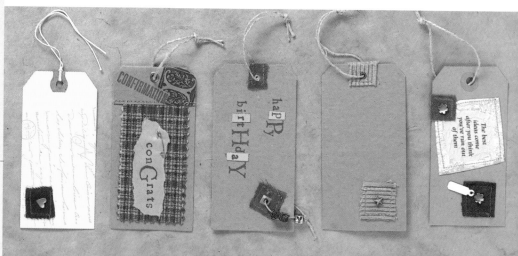

UP the LAZY WEBER
GREAT GRANDPA WALLIN'S CABIN
SOUTH FORK CANYON

summer 2002

few things have brought me closer to my children than sharing my love for grandpa's cabin. I can vividly remember my **childhood** as i watch them throw rocks, ride on the big tree swing and drink from the ice cold spring. I could see the same memories were being re-lived by my mom as we both introduced my children to all the things about the cabin. How thankful i am for the bonds built there — and the traditions that will continue forever!

The tough outdoor look.

how TO

Adhere a large swatch of corduroy to cardstock with fusible web. Add pictures, journaling, and embellishments. Put a small piece of acetate between the leaf and the staple for reinforcement. To make the corduroy "tabs," fold the corduroy over the edge of the cardstock and stitch through all the layers.

how to

To create the corduroy heart accent, cut a heart shape from cardstock. Cut a rectangle around the negative heart image. Next, cut a piece of fabric just smaller than the rectangle. Cut batting to fit inside the heart shape. Then, cut a contrasting piece of cardstock 1/4" larger than your top rectangle (the one with the heart image). Layer the pieces and set with eyelets.

UP THE LAZY WEBER

BY HEIDI SWAPP

VELLUM: Paper Adventures
CORDUROY: Jo-Ann Fabrics
EMBROIDERY FLOSS, TAG, AND EYELETS: Making Memories
PENS: Zig Millennium, Zig Writer (Platinum)
COLORED PENCILS: Prismacolor
CHALKS: Stampin' Up!
COLORED STAPLES: Swingline
LETTERING: Artist's own handwriting
OTHER: Dried leaves

NAPTIME

BY ROBIN JOHNSON

CORDUROY: Jo-Ann Fabrics
FIBERS: On The Surface
HEART: Artist's own design
PENS: Zig Writer
COLORED PENCILS: Prismacolor
EYELETS AND EYELET PLIER: Dritz
METAL LETTERS: Making Memories
LETTERING: Artist's own handwriting

When I was a new mother, I used to get so frustrated when my children reached this stage. They never wanted to take a nap but their little bodies couldn't quite do without one! Often, my kids fell asleep in the late afternoon, woke up at bedtime, and then stayed up half the night. I thought I would go crazy!

Now that I have four children, I have come to realise that every stage is just a stage and that children are more important than schedules.

We love to watch Devin fall asleep sitting upright in a chair. I love to watch the girls giggle as they try to pry his sleepy eyes open. I loved the day i walked up the stairs in the late afternoon and found a little boy snoring in the middle of nowhere...

may 2002

"I am NOT tired and I don't need NAPTIME."

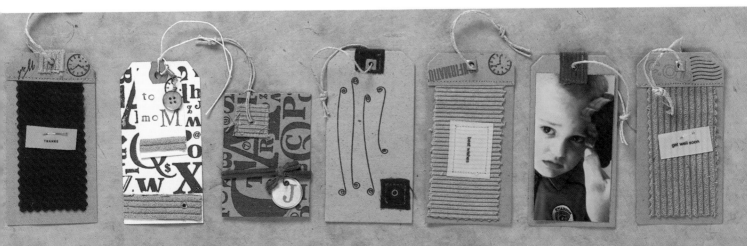

THANKS

to

best wishes

get well soon

woven fabrics

"She who dies with the most fabric wins." Isn't that what the old cliché says? You all probably have heaps of fabric scraps, so use them for tags, borders, book covers, or backgrounds. In this chapter, the artists show how they added texture to their projects with touches of woven fabric. Sort through your stacks of fabric to find treasures that will add texture to your works of art.

how to

Gather all those scraps of heavy fabric and use your rubber stamps to make textured tags. Debbie gives the following suggestions:

- Pink the edges.

- Fold the top edge over and attach a tag to the back to write on, or keep the fabric flat, attach an eyelet, and write on the canvas.

- String a chain or hemp through the eyelets.

- Embroider words or initials or hand stitch your own designs.

- Make several at a time…it'll be difficult to stop!

how to

Cut mat board into three pieces: one for the back and two for the front. (Debbie cut the back piece to 10" x 8 1/4" and the front pieces to 1 3/4" x 8 1/4" and 8 1/4" x 8 1/4".) The narrow strip for the binding piece allows the book to open easily. Stitch copies of your photos onto canvas. Lay the two front pieces side by side, leaving a little space in between. Cover the pieces with the canvas using Diamond Glaze. Decoupage the back piece with canvas and Diamond Glaze, as well. Next, decoupage the inside of the covers with paper. When dry, apply several more coats over the outside and inside to get an even finish. The filler paper is watercolor paper with torn edges. To tear the edges, measure and mark all of your paper, lay a metal ruler along the marked line, and tear to get an even, yet rough edge. Bind with ribbon. Debbie took off the back of the word eyelets with pliers and glued them on with E-6000.

CANVAS THE HOUSE
BY DEBBIE CROUSE

TAGS: American Tag
EYELETS: Dritz
RUBBER STAMPS: Stampers Anonymous (clock and "Wish you were here"), Eclectic Omnibus (alphabet collage)
STAMPING INK: Fabrico
HEMP CORD: Darice
OTHER: Floral rubber stamp, canvas and chains

DORIS
BY DEBBIE CROUSE

MAT BOARD AND WATERCOLOR PAPER: Strathmore
RIBBON: May Arts
CANVAS: Jo-Ann Fabrics
ADHESIVE: Diamond Glaze, JudiKins; E-6000, Eclectic Products
COMPUTER FONT: Cézanne, P22 Type Foundry
EYELETS: Dritz
CHARM: Paper Parachute
BRADS: American Pin & Fastener
WORD EYELETS: Making Memories
METAL NAMEPLATE: Anima Designs

MOM'S QUILT
BY HEIDI SWAPP

COPPER SHEET: Stampendous
TRANSPARENCY: 3M
DATE STAMP: Staples
LETTER STAMPS: Antique Alphabet, PSX Design
INK: StazOn, Tsukineko
OTHER: Burlap, hemp cord, and fabric swatches

getting ready for **DATE NIGHT** *with daddy*

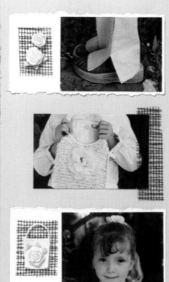

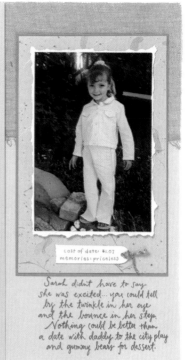

cost of date: $1.07
memories: priceless

Sarah didn't have to say she was excited... you could tell by the twinkle in her eye and the bounce in her step. Nothing could be better than a date with daddy to the city play and gummy bears for dessert.

how to

Mount fabric swatches and photo to cardstock. Cut burlap larger than the cardstock on all sides. Fold over and machine stitch. To create the metal tags, punch copper with a rectangle punch. Leaving a 1/2" border, cut around the rectangle opening. Cut a transparency to fit over the opening and fold the metal over to hold the transparency in place. Punch holes in metal and set with eyelets. Affix to your page with hemp cord. To create the page corners, cut burlap into a square, fold two edges over the corner, and stitch in place.

how TO

When working with fabrics, always check out the selvage; it can add a nice decorative touch. Robin suggests using spray adhesive to adhere the scrim and adhesive dots to adhere the mesh.

DATE NIGHT
BY ROBIN JOHNSON

HANDMADE PAPER: Black Ink
FABRIC: Scrim, Jo-Ann Fabrics
MESH: Magenta
3-D ACCENTS: Jolee's Boutique, Stickopotamus
FIBER: On the Surface
PENS: Zig Writer
CHALKS: Pixie Press
LETTERING: Artist's own handwriting

Organza and silk evoke a feeling of luxury and femininity. When used on your projects, they can create a similar feeling, as Debbie demonstrates on the bridal shower invitation ("Sheer Bliss").

These fabrics can also be used to highlight a focal point. For example, notice how charming Isabella's sweet face is when the rest of the photo is partially obscured with organza. And note how Julie creates a beautiful border and highlights her photo with braided silk on the "Twins" page. This luxurious texture will add an opulent touch to your creations.

baby BETHANY

bethany grace johansen

how to

Before securing the fabric to the page, design your entire layout. Decide which items you would like under the fabric and attach those to your paper. Cut a piece of fabric about 1" larger than the paper. Lay fabric over the top and stitch on all sides. Trim the fabric to the size of your paper with a rotary cutter and a straight edge. Attach the rest of your items on top of the fabric. If the fabric is thick or slick, Robin suggests using Glue Dots for your adhesive.

how to

The pink paper on which the journaling is printed started out as a piece of white cardstock. To create the shimmery color, rub pink Pearl-Ex powder over the white cardstock with your finger. Spray the surface with a matte-finish fixative to prevent the Pearl-Ex from wiping off.

Wrap a mat board frame with silk fabric. The frame is embellished with silk ribbon, braided and tacked on with a stitch in each corner. The little "2" at the top of the page is mounted in a small metal stud. To give it a shiny look, Julie printed the number "2" on cardstock and covered it with a few layers of embossing ink and enamel, heating between layers. **Note**: The stud isn't actually poked through the paper. Julie bent the prongs back and glued it to the page. This prevents your paper from puckering.

2 years old • 2 matching dresses • 2 sweet faces

Judith and Judine Skjoiter

My grandmother lovingly sewed all the clothing worn by my mother and her twin sister. They always looked so cute and stylish. This photo was taken in 1920.

BABY BETHANY
BY ROBIN JOHNSON

FLOWER DIE CUT: Ellison
FLOWER PUNCH: Family Treasures
FABRIC: Shimmery Organza, Pago Fabric Company
INK: Brilliance, Tsukineko
EMBOSSING ENAMEL: Ultra Thick Embossing Enamel, Suze Weinberg
METAL LETTERS AND SNAPS: Making Memories
SQUARE METAL LETTERS: Global Solutions
SILK RIBBON: Bucilla, Plaid
STUDS: Dritz
ADHESIVE: Glue Dots International

TWINS
BY JULIE TURNER

PATTERNED VELLUM: K & Company
SILK FABRIC: Jo-Ann Fabrics
SILK EMBROIDERY RIBBON: Bucilla, Plaid
EMBOSSING INK: Clear Emboss*it*, Ranger Industries
EMBOSSING ENAMEL: Ultra Thick Embossing Enamel, Suze Weinberg
COMPUTER FONT: CK Bella, "The Best of Creative Lettering" CD Combo, *Creating Keepsakes*
FIXATIVE: Krylon
POWDERED PIGMENT: Pearl-Ex, Jacquard Products
OTHER: Metal frame stud and mat board

Cut a piece of organza to 12" x 12". Cut four 2" x 12" strips of vellum. Fold vellum strips in half and cut the ends at an angle to create a mitered corner. Lay the organza over the cardstock. One by one, encase the organza and cardstock in the folded vellum strip and sew through all of the layers. Cut rough holes in the organza and tie back with silk ribbon to expose photos. Heidi also cut a rough hole to expose the ribbon on the tag.

To create the tag, watercolor a piece of watercolor paper and let dry completely. Cut into a tag shape and do your lettering.

ISABELLA
BY HEIDI SWAPP

VELLUM: Autumn Leaves
ORGANZA: Jo-Ann Fabrics
PHOTO CORNERS: Canson
RIBBON: Bucilla, Plaid
WATERCOLORS: Peerless
EYELET: Making Memories
LETTERING: Artist's own handwriting
OTHER: 240 weight watercolor paper & printed paper

SHEER BLISS
BY DEBBIE CROUSE

RIBBON: Midori
ORGANZA: Jo-Ann Fabrics
COMPUTER FONTS: Minstrella ("Heather Hunt"), Times New Roman (address), and Futurist Fixed (details), Microsoft Word

how

Cut an 8 1/2" x 11" sheet of cardstock in half lengthwise. Score and fold a flap up about 2 1/2" from the bottom. Cut a 7 1/2" x 4 1/2" rectangle of organza. Sew the fabric on three sides to the top section of the cardstock, creating a pocket (leave the bottom open). Print insert cards containing shower information and cut to fit the pocket. Fold three pieces of sheer ribbon over the top of the insert and stitch in place. Attach a mini-bow over each ribbon. Insert the card into the organza pocket. Mail in a clear envelope.

4 glass

Take a trip down the halls of a museum and you'll likely find treasured objects encased in glass. Not only does glass provide visual appeal, but it also alludes to the value of an object. Your scrapbook pages and paper art projects have a similar sentimental value, so glass is a perfect texture to use on your pages. Just take care when handling glass because of the sharp edges and corners.

A couple of unlikely glass products you may want to use are glass beads, microscope slides, or mirrors. You can also imitate the illusion of glass with heat embossing, such as Julie uses on her "Waiting" layout.

how to

If you can't find an aged mirror to create texture on your page, you can make your own. Purchase a small mirror from a craft store. Using very fine sandpaper, sand almost the entire finish off the back. You should be able to see through it. Spread Duo Adhesive over the entire back of the mirror. When the glue begins to dry and becomes tacky, cover with silver leafing. Brush off any excess leafing. Mount the mirror on a piece of black paper. The black paper will show through the small holes in the leafing making the mirror look tarnished like an authentic antique mirror.

If you are not comfortable adding glass mirrors to your page, try the mirror-look technique used on the photo frame. Cut a frame from mat board. Dab silver pigment ink over the entire surface of the frame, sprinkle with embossing enamel, and heat emboss. Repeat this process two more times to build up a smooth, glass-like surface. The oval charm hanging from the large silver frame is covered with a layer of glass beads.

how to

Create a personalized shadow box by writing on the glass with a calligraphy dip pen, silver ink, letter stamps and solvent ink.

WAITING
BY JULIE TURNER

PATTERNED PAPER: Anna Griffin
PIGMENT INK: Silver VersaColor, Tsukineko
EMBOSSING ENAMEL: Ultra Thick Embossing Enamel, Suze Weinberg
MIRROR: Michaels
BOW: Anna Griffin
METAL LEAFING: USArtQuest
GLASS BEADS: Gary M. Burlin & Co.
ADHESIVE: Duo Embellishing Adhesive, USArtQuest
COMPUTER FONT: Monet Regular, P22 Type Foundry
OTHER: Frame and metal locket

LIFE IN YOUR YEARS
BY HEIDI SWAPP

CALLIGRAPHY INK: J. Herbin
LETTER STAMPS: PSX Design
STAMPING INK: StazOn, Tsukineko
OTHER: Calligraphy nib & shadow box

MEMORIES UNDER GLASS
BY DEBBIE CROUSE

PRINTED PAPERS: Seven Gypsies
ADHESIVES: Perfect Paper Adhesive, USArtQuest; E-6000, Eclectic Products
STAMPING INK: Van Dyke Brown, Ranger Industries
UTILITY KNIFE: Olfa
GLASS: Home Depot
OTHER: Assorted found objects

MY LITTLE GIRL
BY JULIE TURNER

METAL LEAFING: USArtQuest
ADHESIVE: Duo Embellishing Adhesive, USArtQuest; E-6000, Eclectic Products
COMPUTER FONTS: Dearest Script ("My Little Girl" and "Jillian" tag) and Monet Regular ("Jillian" and "I love you, Dad"), P22 Type Foundry; Abadi (journaling), Word Pro
SILK EMBROIDERY RIBBON: Bucilla
TAG AND EYELETS: Making Memories
OTHER: Glassine envelope, glass from an old picture frame, and a compact disc

how TO

At a home improvement store, have a piece of glass cut to fit snugly inside your box lid. Using a metal ruler and a utility knife, cut a square in the lid. To decoupage the box, begin on the outside and work from the bottom up. Brush an area with a decoupage medium, then cover with bits and pieces of paper. Be sure to cover the top edges of the box by folding the paper over to the inside. Next, line the inside of the box and clean finish the edges. Cover the lid following the same steps. Debbie aged her memory box by lightly dabbing an ink pad over the surface. Let dry for 24 hours, then cover with two more coats of a decoupage medium. Finally, glue the glass into the lid with E-6000.

how to

Select a piece of glass (or Plexiglas) that is larger than the photo that will be covered. A piece of glass from an old 5" x 7" frame works great with 4" x 6" photos. After carefully cleaning the glass, dab all around the border on the back of the glass with Duo Adhesive. When the adhesive is tacky, apply silver leafing. Don't make the glue and leafing appear too solid on the border; it looks best when some of the paper shows through the glass. Adhere the photo to the page, then attach the glass over the photo with a drop of E-6000 glue hidden under each corner. The glue is actually holding the glass to the page; the ribbon tie is only decorative.

For an added touch, Julie burned a CD with the song "My Little Girl," referred to in the journaling. She tucked the CD and a copy of the lyrics into a glassine envelope and tied it to the page.

Jillian,

My little girl, "time flies" is a well worn cliché, but I'm amazed at how fast things happen. One day, I'm holding my red-haired newborn girl in my arms. Now you are very excited that you've started losing your baby teeth, and in a few short years you'll be all grown up. I have a song in my music collection called "My Little Girl." Whenever I listen to it I am reminded of our time together, how precious that time is, and the joy you bring into my life every day.

Mom has tucked the CD behind this page. Whenever you need a reminder of how much I love you, pull it out and listen to the song.

I love you,
Dad

My Little Girl

CLEAR VIEW CARDS

BY DEBBIE CROUSE

ADHESIVES: Mod Podge, Plaid; Aleene's Thick
Tacky Glue, Duncan Enterprises
GLASS SLIDES: Manto Fev
DRIED FLOWERS: Nature's Pressed

how to

Cut pictures to fit under a glass slide. Index
prints are the perfect size for this project.
Brush Mod Podge over the pictures and place
on a slide. Take care not to get Mod Podge on
the part of the glass that is not over an object
or picture or it will show through the glass.
Allow to dry for 24 hours. When dry, adhere
the slide to the card using Tacky Glue. Any flat
object can be used in place of a picture, such
as dried flowers or paper.

Or what John Lennon wrote before he was gunned down in the driveway of the Dakota: "Life is what happens to you while you're busy making other plans."

summer 2002

Before securing the transparency to the page, complete the background page first. Cut a hole in the transparency where the photo will be. Dab clear embossing ink around the opening and heat emboss with colored embossing powder. Heidi also added more texture by tearing the transparency. Write on the transparency using a calligraphy dip pen and silver calligraphy ink. When dry, attach the transparency to the layout with eyelets.

Spray the back of a piece of glass with adhesive and adhere the tag strings and a quotation. Then adhere the glass to your page with E-6000.

CHERISH NOW
BY HEIDI SWAPP

HANDMADE PAPER: Black Ink
ADHESIVE: E-6000, Eclectic Products
TRANSPARENCY: 3M
EMBOSSING POWDER: Ranger Industries
EMBOSSING INK: Clear Emboss*it*, Ranger Industries
TAG: Making Memories
TAG AND EYELETS: Making Memories
OTHER: Calligraphy ink, calligraphy nib, and a piece of glass

PEACH ON THE BEACH
BY HEIDI SWAPP

PATTERNED PAPER: Papers by Katherine
EMBROIDERY FLOSS: DMC
PENS: Zig Millennium
LETTER STAMPS: PSX Design
BRASS FRAME: Ink It!
GLASS BEADS: Gary M. Burlin & Co.
ADHESIVE: Wonder Tape, Suze Weinberg; Diamond Glaze, JudiKins
LETTERING: Artist's own handwriting

Adhere a frame to your page. Place a photo in the frame, fill with Diamond Glaze, and allow to set overnight.

To put glass beads on a picture, cut a Wonder Tape sheet to the size of the photo. Peel off the white side of the Wonder Tape. Position the tape over the photo and smooth out any wrinkles. Remove the pink covering from the Wonder Tape. Pour on glass beads and press onto the adhesive. Pour off any extra beads. As a final touch to her layout, Heidi pre-punched holes and stitched a zigzag border around selected elements. **Note:** Carefully plan your stitching so it comes out evenly.

5 plastic

When Leo Baekeland developed plastic back in the early 1900s, little did he know that paper artists would later use it as a design element. In this chapter, our artists creatively put his invention to good use and prove that plastic measures up to its advertising slogan as being a "material of 1,000 uses." For example, Heidi cleverly uses a CD-case to protect a mini-book, and Julie ingeniously displays the bits and pieces of nature her children collected from Grandpa's forest. Debbie shows us another use as she encloses personalized memorabilia in plastic pockets ("Pocket Cards"). Have fun thinking of creative uses for this durable material!

how TO *Shrink Plastic*

Cut a tag from a piece of shrink plastic and punch an 1/8" hole at the top. Keep in mind that the shrink plastic will shrink to less than half its original size. Handwrite your journaling on the tag using a pen that will adhere to plastic (a Sharpie or Slick Writer) or trace a computer font. To trace a font, print your text onto a sheet of paper. Place it under the plastic tag and carefully trace the text with the pen. Remember the writing will also shrink to less than half its original size. Shrink the plastic according to the manufacturer's directions.

To achieve the shiny, "ocean spray" look for your background, dab clear embossing ink all over a transparency and heat emboss with clear embossing enamel. Lightly sprinkle the bumpy surface with white embossing enamel and heat it from the bottom so the sprinkles of white don't blow away.

how to *Stamp Plastic*

Cut a piece of clear shrink plastic to 8" x 8". Lightly sand the back of the plastic with very fine sandpaper. Rub light blue chalk all over the sanded surface. Shrink the plastic at the temperature recommended on the package. To make an impression in the frame, firmly press a boldly patterned stamp into the hot plastic immediately after pulling the shrunken plastic from the oven. Heating the plastic slightly longer than recommended can make it easier to imprint. After the plastic has cooled, accent the raised areas on the front of the frame by gently wiping them with a light-colored Rub-On. Spray with a fixative. The frames can be used as a background for journaling or small photos.

PLAYING IN GRANDPA'S FOREST

BY JULIE TURNER

WOOD VENEER: Lenderlink Technologies, Inc.
SLIDE POCKET PAGE: Vue-All, Inc.
EMBOSSABLE PLASTIC: Gary M. Burlin & Co.
BRADS: Impress Rubber Stamps
EYELETS: Coffee Break Designs
TAGS: Making Memories and American Tag
LETTER STAMPS: PSX Design (Antique Alphabet), PrintWorks (large)
WATCH CRYSTAL: Deluxe Plastic Arts
SHRINK PLASTIC: PolyShrink, Lucky Squirrel
STAMPING INK: Black 213, Ranger Industries
EMBOSSING ENAMEL: Ultra Thick Embossing Enamel, Suze Weinberg
EMBOSSING INK: Clear Emboss*it*, Ranger Industries
FONT: Typewriter, P22 Type Foundry

HITTING THE SURF

BY JULIE TURNER

SHRINK PLASTIC: PolyShrink, Lucky Squirrel
PEN: Slick Writer, American Crafts
TRANSPARENCY: 3M (for laser printers)
EMBOSSING INK: Clear Emboss*it*, Ranger Industries
EMBOSSING ENAMEL: Ultra Thick Embossing Enamel, Suze Weinberg
EYELETS: Making Memories
EMBROIDERY FLOSS: DMC
FONT: CK Hustle, "Fresh Fonts" CD, *Creating Keepsakes*

LAKESIDE LUAU

BY JULIE TURNER

PATTERNED PAPER: Magenta
SHRINK PLASTIC: PolyShrink, Lucky Squirrel
RUBBER STAMPS: All Night Media, (imprint on shrink plastic); PSX Design (Antique Alphabet)
CHALK AND RUB-ONS: Craf-T Products
SPRAY FIXATIVE: Krylon
FIBERS: Rubba Dub Dub, Art Sanctum
BEADS: Designs by Pamela
EYELETS: Making Memories
COMPUTER FONTS: Garamouche, P22 Type Foundry

SANTA INEZ

BY HEIDI SWAPP

PRINTED PAPER: Anna Griffin
FIBERS: Adornaments, K1C2
PENS: Zig Millennium
LETTER STAMPS: PSX Design
STAMPING INK: Brilliance, Tsukineko
CHARMS: Designs by Pamela
SNAP: Dritz
ETCHING PAINT: White Frost, Delta
PAPER BAG: Creative Imaginations
ADHESIVE: Glue Dots International
OTHER: CD-case, twine, foam core, and hemp cord

how to

Julie enclosed bits of nature in a slide pocket page, attached to wood veneer with brads. The slide pockets were a bit too wide for an 8 1/2" x 11" page, so she stitched a new, narrower side seam on each side and trimmed off a little of the plastic. Try using this technique to showcase beachcombing treasures, vacation souvenirs, and baby or wedding memorabilia.

The word strips in the "rock pocket" and under the watch crystal were made from shrink plastic. Lightly sand strips of white shrink plastic to make the inks adhere better. Ink over the entire surface with colored ink, stamp with letter stamps, and shrink according to the directions on the package. Use a small amount of E-6000 to attach the plastic watch crystal. The letter "t" (on the top row) is stamped and heat embossed on a small rock.

how TO

To make the mini-book, fold a 4 1/2" x 10 5/8" piece of paper in half. Hand stitch in the fold with embroidery floss to bind the pages. Embellish as desired. Cut a square the size of the CD-case in the foam core, adding an extra 1/4" on the left side to allow the case to open. Adhere a piece of cardstock to the back of the foam core. To create the image on the CD-case, tape off an area to etch. Paint on white frost paint and let dry. Stamp an image onto the painted area. Insert the CD-case into the cutout of the foam core and adhere to the cardstock backing with adhesive dots or double-sided tape.

Pocket cards are a perfect way to personalize a card for a friend or family member. With a little planning, you'll have fun creating this card! First, plan out how many pockets you want on the card—odd numbers work best. Gather small, flat objects that relate to the person to whom you'll give the card. Cut a sheet protector to the desired overall size. Machine stitch the sides and bottom to the cardstock. Then, for the nine-section card, sew two vertical lines, creating three even columns. Fill the bottom three sections with your objects, then sew just above the objects to close. Fill the other sections in the same manner. For the seven-section card, sew the sides and bottom. Measure and sew the vertical columns. Fill with chosen objects and sew across the top. "Make several of these cards at once," Debbie suggests, "because they are fun to do, and once you have the supplies out, they go together quickly."

CROUSE KIDS— UNMATCHED
BY DEBBIE CROUSE

WAXED LINEN: Darice
LETTER STAMPS: Carved in Stone Alphabet, Inkadinkado
STAMPING INK: Black, Memories
EMBOSSING INK: Clear Emboss*it*, Ranger Industries
EMBOSSING ENAMEL: Ultra Thick Embossing Enamel, Suze Weinberg
BRADS: Magic Scraps
NAME PLATE: Anima Designs
SLIDE POCKET PAGE: Savage Paper Products

POCKET CARDS
BY DEBBIE CROUSE

STAMPING INK: Van Dyke Brown, Ranger Industries
EYELETS: Making Memories
GLASS HEARTS: Mill Hill
UTILITY KNIFE: Olfa
OTHER: Sheet protector and assorted found objects

Cut a vertical strip from a slide pocket page. Fold cardstock into the shape of a matchbook. Staple the slide pocket strip to the inside of the matchbook to create an accordion-fold display. On the mini-tag, which is stapled to the matchbook, stamp letters and heat emboss. Attach the name plate with brads. This matchbook would make an ideal gift for a proud grandma!

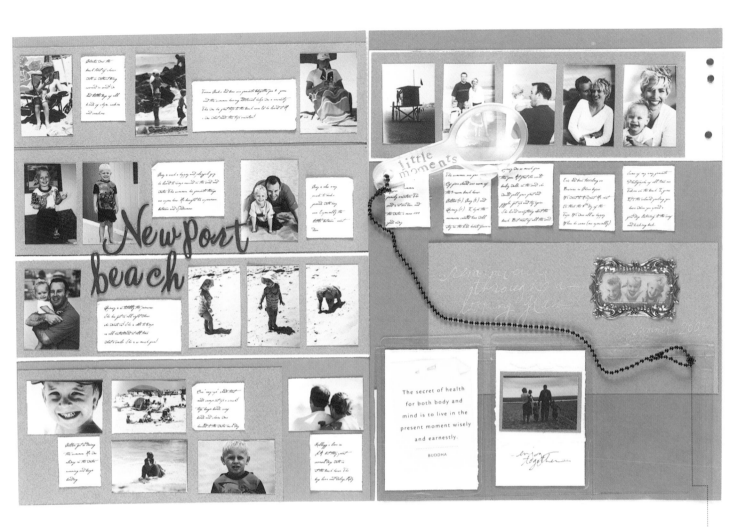

Arrange six photos on a piece of 12" x 12" cardstock and photograph in natural light. After getting the pictures developed, cut them out and arrange on your layout. Print your journaling in the smallest font and add to your page. To distress the journaling blocks, lightly chalk each block and scratch the edges with your fingernail after it has been adhered to the page. Cut out pockets from a plastic pocket page and attach them to the outside of your page protector with double-sided tape. Place selected photos or journaling in laminated pouches and put inside the pockets. Heidi included a magnifying glass in one of the pockets to make reading the miniature font easier and more fun.

The secret of health for both body and mind is to live in the present moment wisely and earnestly.

BUDDHA

NEWPORT BEACH— LITTLE MOMENTS

BY HEIDI SWAPP

BLACK CHAIN: Coffee Break Designs
LETTER STAMPS: PSX Design
STAMPING INK: StazOn, Tsukineko
METAL LETTERS: Making Memories
MAGNIFYING GLASS: The C-Thru Ruler Company
MINI BLACK BRADS: Lost Art, American Tag
FONT: Cézanne, P22 Type Foundry
LAMINATING CARDS: 3M
POCKET PAGE: Print File
DOUBLE-SIDED TAPE: Magic Scraps
ADHESIVE: Diamond Glaze, JudiKins
OTHER: Frame, calligraphy nibs, and calligraphy ink

6 transparencies

Transparencies aren't just for teachers anymore! Now they're used by scrapbookers, card-makers, and crafters. Since this material is obviously transparent, it's quite versatile and can be altered to fit almost any project. Take a look and see how the artists use transparencies as an overlay, a photo frame, or a pocket.

Here are some helpful hints when working with transparencies. Rubber stamp on the transparency using solvent ink so it adheres to the slick surface. Heavier weight transparencies used for laser copiers are ideal for rubber-stamping and heat embossing. To print on a transparency, use the ones made for ink jet printers, mirror the image or text, and print on the rough side so you can view the image from the smooth side. Transparencies come in multi-packs, but if you want just a sheet or two, stores such as Kinko's sell it by the sheet.

SARAH AND PATCH
BY ROBIN JOHNSON

FOAM CORE AND DATE STAMP: Office Max
TRANSPARENCY: 3M
PENS: EK Success
STAMPING INK: Tsukineko
SNAPS AND CIRCLE LETTERS: Making Memories
STUDS: Dritz
WATERCOLOR PENCILS: Derwent
LETTERING: Artist's own handwriting

how TO

To make the book, cut two 12" x 12" sheets in half. Score in half and fold. Machine stitch the center fold. For the cover, color copy a picture in the black and white mode onto a transparency. Write your text on the cover, then secure the transparency to the cover with snaps. The foam core also has a transparency secured in place with brads pushed into the foam core. This holds the book in place but lets you see through it.

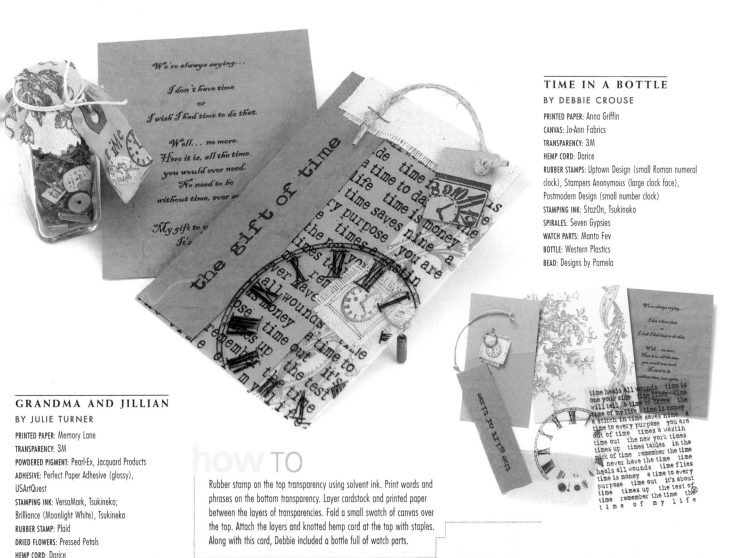

TIME IN A BOTTLE
BY DEBBIE CROUSE

PRINTED PAPER: Anna Griffin
CANVAS: Jo-Ann Fabrics
TRANSPARENCY: 3M
HEMP CORD: Darice
RUBBER STAMPS: Uptown Design (small Roman numeral clock), Stampers Anonymous (large clock face), Postmodern Design (small number clock)
STAMPING INK: StazOn, Tsukineko
SPIRALES: Seven Gypsies
WATCH PARTS: Manto Fev
BOTTLE: Western Plastics
BEAD: Designs by Pamela

GRANDMA AND JILLIAN
BY JULIE TURNER

PRINTED PAPER: Memory Lane
TRANSPARENCY: 3M
POWDERED PIGMENT: Pearl-Ex, Jacquard Products
ADHESIVE: Perfect Paper Adhesive (glossy), USArtQuest
STAMPING INK: VersaMark, Tsukineko; Brilliance (Moonlight White), Tsukineko
RUBBER STAMP: Plaid
DRIED FLOWERS: Pressed Petals
HEMP CORD: Darice
TAG: American Tag
OTHER: Buttons, charms

how TO

Rubber stamp on the top transparency using solvent ink. Print words and phrases on the bottom transparency. Layer cardstock and printed paper between the layers of transparencies. Fold a small swatch of canvas over the top. Attach the layers and knotted hemp cord at the top with staples. Along with this card, Debbie included a bottle full of watch parts.

how to

Mix one part Pearl-Ex with six parts Perfect Paper Adhesive to make a sheer paint. Paint the mixture onto a transparency. When dry, cut to desired mat size.

The swirl borders were made with a stamp and watermark stamp pad. The tag on the bottom right was lightly rubbed with a white ink pad.

Heidi wanted the book to be low profile and open flat, so she created a folio cover for the pages and slipped the pages inside. To create a similar folio, cut two pieces of cardstock to the same size. Those will become the front and back of the folio. For the binding, cut a piece of paper twice the width you want showing on the font, then fold it in half. Sew one of the pieces of cardstock to half of the binding strip and, if you want, add a seam line 1/4" inside your original stitching for looks. Sew the second piece of cardstock to the other half of the binding. Next, sew corners onto the front. For the label holder, cut paper to desired size and cut a rectangle from the center. Stitch around the inside rectangle and across the top of the label holder before sewing it to the cover, so the top remains open. Add a piece of transparency to form a window. Paint walnut ink onto the exposed cardstock on the front of the folio.

For the inside pages, also called a "signature," cut cardstock to desired size. Heidi suggests using no more than five pages. Determine the type of pocket you want on each page, then cut and sew a transparency according to your plan. Stitch the pages together with a zigzag stitch on the left-hand side. Fold back each page just to the right of the stitching to establish a crease.

To make the book low profile, sew a 1" x 8" transparency strip to the inside back cover near the binding. The last page of her "book" slides into the transparency strip to hold the pages in place. You can add another signature to your folio by adding another transparency strip.

Heidi offers the following tips for creating your own folio:

- Create a "storyboard" to plan your journaling, photos, and embellishments.

- Add memorabilia on the back of each page to cover the stitching.

- Use double-stick tape to affix label tabs.

- Age the tags by brushing them with walnut ink.

- Tuck photos and tags containing additional information and journaling into pockets.

- To create the window in the envelope, cut open the envelope down one side and the bottom. Cut out the desired size for the window and sew a transparency piece on the inside. Finally, glue the envelope back together.

PROJECT DESERT

BY HEIDI SWAPP

PAPER: Black Ink
TRANSPARENCY: 3M
TAGS: Artist's own design
REINFORCEMENTS AND FILE TABS: Avery
STAPLES: Swingline
CLEAR BAGS: Impact Images
RUB-ONS: Craf-T Products
WALNUT INK: Postmodern Design
LETTER STAMPS: PSX Design
STAMPING INK: StazOn, Tsukineko
COMPUTER FONT: Hootie, downloaded from the Internet
FIBERS: Rubba Dub Dub, Art Sanctum
OTHER: Envelopes and hemp cord

EMERGENCY
BY ROBIN JOHNSON

FOAM CORE: Office Max
TRANSPARENCY: 3M
ADHESIVE: Perfect Paper Adhesive, USArtQuest
TAG: American Tag
HATCHET: Just Joshin'
COMPUTER FONT: Impact
OTHER: Hershey's Chocolate

WILL
BY DEBBIE CROUSE

TRANSPARENCY: 3M
CANVAS: Jo-Ann Fabrics
BUTTON: Making Memories
PAINT SAMPLE: Home Depot

THANK YOU
BY DEBBIE CROUSE

TRANSPARENCY: 3M
HEMP CORD: Darice
ADHESIVE: Glue Dots International
RUBBER STAMPS: Savvy Stamps ("thank you"), Hero Arts (French Script), Limited Edition (mail and tag stamps)
STAMPING INK: StazOn, Tsukineko
TAG: American Tag
WATCH FACE: Manto Fev
OTHER: Fabric swatches and chipboard

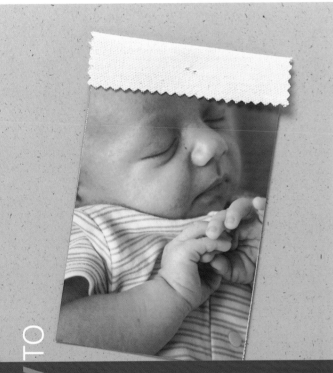

how to

Xerox copy baby information onto a transparency. Cut the paint chip and transparency to the size of your photo. Sew a button on the top of the canvas to attach all of the layers together. Debbie comments, "It was a bonus that the colors I liked had names that were appropriate for this project."

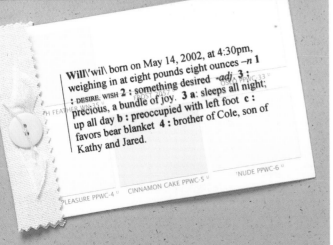

Will\'wil\ born on May 14, 2002, at 4:30pm, weighing in at eight pounds eight ounces *—n* **1** : DESIRE, WISH **2** : something desired *—adj.* **3** : precious, a bundle of joy. **3 a** : sleeps all night; up all day **b** : preoccupied with left foot **c** : favors bear blanket **4** : brother of Cole, son of Kathy and Jared.

how to

Cut chipboard and transparencies to desired size. Rubber stamp on the transparencies. Layer fabric swatches and ephemera under the transparencies and bundle them all together with hemp cord.

Debbie loved the idea of having almost no adhesive for this thank you card. The only adhesive she used was an adhesive dot under the watch face. Debbie suggests, "Just bundle it all up under the transparency, slip your message in the back under the transparency, and you're done. It's fast and easy!"

IN CASE OF EMERGENCY
BREAK GLASS

how to

Cut two layers of foam core to desired size and adhere together. Glue a piece of cardstock to the top of the foam core. Cut a hole in the center through all of the layers. Adhere foam core to a piece of cardstock for the backing. Affix chocolate to backing, then adhere a transparency on the top. Print your text onto another piece of cardstock, cut out the center, and adhere over the top of the transparency. Embellish with hatchet and tag.

chipboard&cardboard

Grab part of a cardboard box or the rigid packaging from a man's dress shirt and you'll have the ideal supplies to create a timeless, rugged-looking project. Chipboard and cardboard, which are so readily available, have a neutral color that can be adapted to any color scheme. In addition, you can use these "recycled" materials to make a background page, tag, or photo mat. The possibilities are endless! Don't forget to spray chipboard and cardboard with Archival Mist before adhering your photos to them.

SANTA BARBARA
BY JULIE TURNER

POWDERED PIGMENT: Pearl-Ex, Super Bronze and Antique Gold, Jacquard Products
EYELET WORDS AND NUMBERS: Making Memories
LETTER STAMPS: The Missing Link Stamp Co.
CHALK: Craf-T Products
ADHESIVE: Perfect Paper Adhesive, USArtQuest
TAG: American Tag
HEMP CORD: Darice
COMPUTER FONT: CK Corral, "Fresh Fonts" CD, *Creating Keepsakes*
OTHER: Chipboard

TAG SALE
BY DEBBIE CROUSE

TAG DIE CUTS: Accu-Cut and Ellison
RUBBER STAMPS: Hero Arts (French script, flower, bike stamp, and Paraguay), Eclectic Omnibus (random letters), Hampton Art Stamps (eye), Stampa Rosa (postal cancellation and Paris postmark), PSX Design (Antique Alphabet), Inkadinkado (Carved in Stone Alphabet), Sanford Corporation (C.O.D., Parcel Post, Confirmation)
STAMPING INK: Black, Memories; Van Dyke Brown, Ranger Industries
UTILITY KNIFE: Olfa
EYELETS, METAL LETTERS, AND CHARMS: Making Memories
LIBRARY CARD SLEEVE: Silver Crow Creations
OTHER: Chipboard and corduroy

how to

Die cut two identical tags. Cut a window in one of the tags with a utility cutter and metal ruler. Rubber stamp as desired. Sew a piece of plastic from a sheet protector in the window. Sew the two tags together, stitching around the outer edges of the tags, leaving the short end open for inserting a message or ephemera. These would make unique luggage tags.

For the "See You in Two Weeks" card, slip one of the tags into a library sleeve, then adhere onto a card.

how to

To create the photo mats, mix a small amount of Super Bronze Pearl-Ex and Perfect Paper Adhesive to make paint. Haphazardly paint the mixture onto torn chipboard. For the darker flecks, mix Antique Gold Pearl-Ex with Perfect Paper and fleck onto chipboard with a toothbrush.

Julie aged the journaling blocks with chalk.

Our entire Turner clan stopped for a tour of the mission at Santa Barbara on our way up the California coast. 7/2001

Cousins Jeremy, Jillian, Jackson, John and Jennifer.

santa Barbara

how TO

Scribble on the chipboard with a white watercolor crayon. Lightly smear with a wet paintbrush. Scribble over the surface again with the watercolor crayon.

The bottom left square is actually a mini-book that opens to reveal Julie's journaling. To create the book, cut two pieces of chipboard to the same size. Cut an opening in one of the squares with an X-Acto knife. Bind the pieces of chipboard together with a small strip of folded paper that acts as a hinge. Mount a photo on a Making Memories tag.

how to

To create the chipboard embellishment, stamp an image onto a rectangle piece of chipboard. Place a dictionary definition on the chipboard and cover with matte Perfect Paper Adhesive. When dry, age the chipboard by bending and manipulating it. Set an eyelet at the top and bottom and affix it to the cover with knotted hemp cord strung through the eyelets.

For the book, cut three pages of 12" x 12" cardstock in half, then fold in half. Punch two holes along the fold and bind with hemp cord by running the hemp through the holes twice then tying several macramé knots.

PLAYMATES, CLASSMATES, ROOMMATES

BY JULIE TURNER

WATERCOLOR CRAYONS: Staedtler
TAG: Making Memories (vellum), American Tag (circle)
LETTER STAMPS: Barnes & Noble (large), PSX Design (Antique Alphabet)
STAMPING INK: Charcoal Grey, Ranger Industries
COMPUTER FONT: Garamouche, P22 Type Foundry
CORNER ROUNDER: Lassco Products
PEWTER WORDS AND NUMBER: Making Memories
EYELETS: Making Memories (large), Coffee Break Designs (small)
OTHER: Chipboard

SAN FRANSCISCO MINI-BOOK

BY HEIDI SWAPP

RUBBER STAMPS: Stampin' Up! (column); Alphabet Set (architectural), Diffusion Series, Hampton Art Stamps; JudiKins (postal); Hero Arts (alphabet blocks and French script); Uptown Design (hotel postmark)
STAMPING INK: Ancient Page, Clearsnap
TAG: American Tag
SNAPS AND EYELET: Making Memories
POSTAGE STAMPS: Stampa Rosa
OTHER: Film negative, dictionary definition, staples, and hemp cord

COMPETITION
DETERMINATION
COMMITMENT

ALL·STARS

JUNE 2002

"put it in the glove"

glove

When using cardboard as a background, cut an extra 1/4" off the height and width so it fits in your page protector. For a rugged look, peel off part of the cardboard to expose the corrugation.

how to

Cut two circles out of cardstock 1/2" wider than the toilet paper roll. Get them really wet, then squeeze out excess water. Form around the ends of the roll and secure with hemp. Be sure to put your invitation inside before closing the second end. As the cardstock dries, it will conform to the roll. To make the "puddle," adhere your title to the outside of the roll. Stamp embossing ink over the title, pour on embossing enamel, and heat emboss.

This invitation could also be used for a slumber party (bring your own roll of toilet paper), a treasure or scavenger hunt, or a safari party.

PUT IT IN THE GLOVE
BY HEIDI SWAPP

BASEBALL ACCENTS: K & Company
PHOTO CORNERS: Canson
LETTERING: Artist's own handwriting
OTHER: Star studs and cardboard

A WEE INVITATION
BY DEBBIE CROUSE

HEMP CORD: Darice
LETTER STAMPS: Inkadinkado (Carved in Stone Alphabet), PSX Design (Antique Alphabet)
EMBOSSING INK: Clear Emboss*it*, Ranger Industries
EMBOSSING ENAMEL: Ultra Thick Embossing Enamel, Suze Weinberg
OTHER: Toilet paper roll

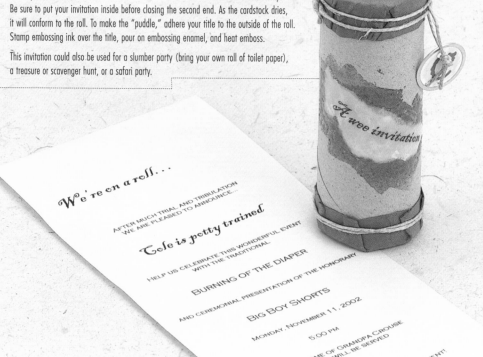

A wee invitation

We're on a roll...

AFTER MUCH TRIAL AND TRIBULATION
WE ARE PLEASED TO ANNOUNCE...

Cole is potty trained

HELP US CELEBRATE THIS WONDERFUL EVENT
WITH THE TRADITIONAL

BURNING OF THE DIAPER

AND CEREMONIAL PRESENTATION OF THE HONORARY

BIG BOY SHORTS

MONDAY, NOVEMBER 11, 2002

5:00 PM

HOME OF GRANDPA CROUSE
DINNER WILL BE SERVED

EVENT

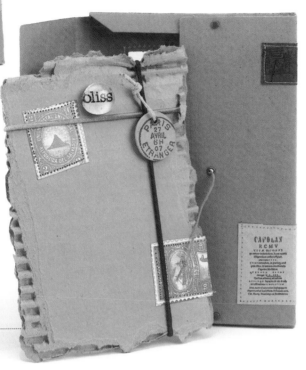

PATTERNED PAPER: Anna Griffin

DIE CUTS: Ellison

HEMP CORD: Darice

RUBBER STAMPS: Limited Edition Rubber Stamps (Mail and Tag Art Set), Stampa Rosa ("Wish You Were Here" and Paris postmark)

STAMPING INK: Van Dyke Brown, Ranger Industries

EYELETS: E-Z Set

BRADS: American Tag

HAIR ELASTICS: Nordstrom Rack

OTHER: Sheet protector, chipboard, and cardboard

CORY PAUL
BY HEIDI SWAPP

METAL CHAIN: Coffee Break Designs

RUBBER STAMPS: Staples (date), JudiKins (dragon), Stampa Rosa (postage cancellation), Rubber Baby (letters), Stampers Anonymous (label holder)

STAMPING INK: Ancient Page, Clearsnap

CHINESE COIN: Hong Kong

METAL STUD: Diane Ribbon and Notion Co.

OTHER: Dog tag and postage stamp

how to

Die cut an envelope from chipboard. Use a square or rectangle-shaped die to cut out a window for the plastic inset. Cut a sheet protector 3/4" larger than the window. While the envelope is flat, sew plastic over the window and embellish by topstitching patches of stamped and aged paper onto the envelope. Fold envelope and close sides with brads.

For the card insert, tear corrugated cardboard to fit inside the envelope and embellish.

how TO

For the background, wet cardstock and crinkle. Iron to dry. Paint with walnut ink and iron to dry again, putting a piece of paper between your iron and the cardstock. Sand various places to expose the original cardstock color.

To create the chipboard embellishment, scan the thesaurus entry, print onto paper, and tear around the edges. Decoupage the torn paper to the chipboard. Add stamps and other ephemera. Distress the chipboard by bending the corners and adding Rub-Ons to the edges, then machine stitch it to the background paper using black thread.

8 metal

Sturdy, sleek, and malleable, metal can add magnificent texture to your projects. And metal doesn't have to be the traditional metallic color; you can use copper sheets, add a matte finish to aluminum sheets, or even create the appearance of metal with plastic and paint. Notice how the artists have used metal to create depth and interest on their works of art.

how to

Heidi engraved on the metal with a stylus. To achieve the raised letters, you must do your lettering from the back. Write your word on a piece of vellum and position the vellum face down on the back of the copper sheet (you'll be tracing the word backwards). Do your writing on a soft surface such as a mouse pad. You may have to trace over your word a couple of times to get a strong image.

To age the copper, mix 1 cup of water with 1 tablespoon of liver of sulfur. (Do this technique outside or in a well-ventilated area.) Bathe the copper in the mixture for a few seconds. The copper will turn completely black. Rub with steel wool until you are satisfied with the look.

Create the windows in the copper sheet by lightly marking the openings with a stylus and cutting them out with a pair of old scissors. Cut a small angled slit in each corner, fold back the metal an 1/8", and hammer down.

TOUGHNESS
BY HEIDI SWAPP

EYELETS: Making Memories
BRADS: Lost Art, American Tag
ADHESIVE: Perfect Paper Adhesive, USArtQuest
COPPER SHEET AND LIVER OF SULFUR: Maid-o'-Metal, St. Louis Crafts
LEATHER STAMPS: Leather Factory

HEAVY METAL
BY DEBBIE CROUSE

PATTERNED PAPER: Seven Gypsies and K & Company
WAXED LINEN: Darice
ADHESIVE: PVA, Books by Hand; Diamond Glaze, JudiKins; Mod Podge, Plaid
AWL: Making Memories
WATCH PARTS: Manto Fev
METAL MINI FRAMES: Ink It!
BOTTLE: Darice
ASSORTED HARDWARE: Home Depot
COPPER AND ALUMINUM SHEETS: Maid-o'-Metal, St. Louis Crafts
JUMP RINGS: Darice
OTHER: Wire cutters, round needle nose pliers, 20-gauge wire, and metal frame studs

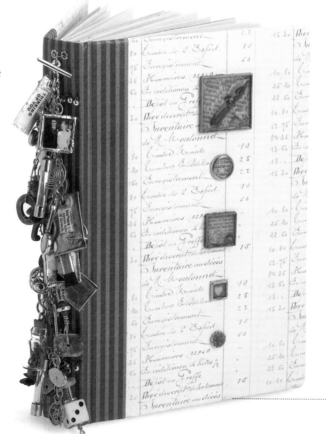

how to

This book is patterned after a technique called "junque book" taught in a class at Memory Lane. Remove the insides of an old book. Using PVA, cover the book as shown in the aging chapter, but add a strip of paper over the spine. Fill your book with several signatures by attaching them through the spine. The frames on the front cover are backed with dictionary definitions, filled with assorted found objects, then covered with Diamond Glaze.

Set two eyelets on both ends of the spine. Attach a charm bracelet through the eyelets with wire. Debbie attached a plethora of charms to the bracelet. She made the charms from found objects in her jewelry box, junk drawer, toolbox, button box, or whatever she could find. She even got out the soldering iron and put jump rings on fuses and on a mini picture charm. To make the copper tags, punch a rectangle window into a copper sheet, through which a word or picture will show. With your word or picture showing through the hole, wrap the copper around a piece of chipboard or mat board and set an eyelet. Debbie recommends that you just get creative! You can use buttons, beads, springs, charms, watch parts, nuts, and anything else you find. Using your needle nose pliers and silver wire, have fun twisting and wrapping to make funky shapes.

how TO

Prepare the metal for journaling by giving it a matte finish. After cutting metal to desired size, apply a layer of matte-finish Perfect Paper. Quick dry with an embossing gun. To rubber stamp on a photo or glossy surface, use inks that are specially designed for slick surfaces.

how to

The embellishments on this page look like real pieces of tin ceiling, but they are actually plastic dollhouse trim that was painted to create an authentic tin ceiling look. Paint the shiny white plastic with a very thin coat of watered-down white acrylic paint, giving it a matte, aged finish. When dry, lightly rub the raised areas with Rub-Ons. The other raised embellishments are cream-colored dollhouse trims that Julie cut to fit her layout and glued on with a dab of E-6000. **Artist's tip:** Julie threaded the silk embroidery ribbon on a ribbon needle, which has a long, narrow eye, making it easier to string the beads and sew on her page.

BONJOUR PARIS

BY ROBIN JOHNSON

PRINTED PAPER: Autumn Leaves
METAL COINS: Treasures & Trinkets
LETTER STAMPS: PSX Design
STAMPING INK: Brillance, Tsukineko
BRADS AND LABEL HOLDERS: Making Memories
CUT-OUTS: Fresh Cuts, EK Success
SHEET METAL: Metal Works, Lefranc & Bourgeois
ADHESIVE: Perfect Paper Adhesive (matte), USArtQuest

BEAUTIFUL BALLERINAS

BY JULIE TURNER

PRINTED PAPER: Anna Griffin
SILK EMBROIDERY RIBBON: Bucilla
BEADS: Designs by Pamela
COMPUTER FONT: Dearest, P22 Type Foundry
EMBOSSING POWDER: Platinum, Ranger Industries
TIN CEILING AND MOLDINGS: Houseworks
PAINT: White Acrylic, Liquitex
RUB-ONS: Craf-T Products

Run your hand over a screen door and your senses will be tickled with texture. When used on paper arts, the same tactile experience can occur. As illustrated with these projects, screen can be used for a masculine, hardy look or for a fancy, feminine feel.

how to

Fold a piece of cardstock over the screen and secure all layers with a staple. Hang elements from the screen with jump rings.

EXTREME

BY HEIDI SWAPP

DOG TAGS: Chronicle Books
TAGS: American Tag
METAL LETTERS: Making Memories
COMPUTER FONT: John Doe, downloaded from Internet
LETTER STAMPS: Antique Alphabet, PSX Design
STAMPING INK: Brilliance, Tsukineko
OTHER: Staples, jump rings, and screen

BIG BOYS

BY ROBIN JOHNSON

MODELING PASTE: Liquitex
STAMPING INK: Fresco, Stampa Rosa
LETTER STAMPS: All Night Media (Ransom), PrintWorks (lowercase)
WIRE MESH: American Art Clay Co.
HARDWARE: From Robin's junk drawer

how TO

For the border on the left page, punch holes in the screen to create spaces for the 3-D objects. To avoid sharp edges on the border, wrap the screen to the back of your cardstock and adhere the ends with tape. Create the title by smearing modeling paste on your paper with a palette knife, making it as smooth as possible. Wait until the modeling paste is nearly dry, then press inked stamps into the paste.

Cut screen twice as long as you want your card. Cut 1" strips from assorted papers to go around the edges of the screen. Fold the strips in half lengthwise and sew them onto the screen, overlapping the ends of the strips. Now fold the screen in half to make the card. Tie on seam binding and attach sentiments, pictures, and fabric squares with pins and ties. The inside sentiment says, "Happiness often sneaks through a door you didn't know you left open."

Debbie thinks the best part about this card is that you can see all the way through it. She was pleasantly surprised that sewing on the screen was not a problem. If you don't have access to a sewing machine, you can leave the edges raw.

PIN UP
BY DEBBIE CROUSE

PAPER: Anna Griffin, Bravissimo, and Seven Gypsies
SCREEN: Lowe's
OTHER: Seam binding

RENDEZVOUS
BY JULIE TURNER

SCREEN: Lowe's
TAG: American Tag
METAL TAG: Magic Scraps
LETTER STAMPS: Carved in Stone, Inkadinkado
STAMPING INK: Black 213, Ranger Industries; ColorBox Fluid Chalk, Clearsnap
EMBOSSING ENAMEL: Ultra Thick Embossing Enamel, Suze Weinberg
EMBOSSING INK: Clear Emboss*it*, Ranger Industries
EYELETS AND BRADS: Making Memories
CHAIN: Coffee Break Designs
COMPUTER FONT: CK Carbon Copy, "Fresh Fonts" CD, *Creating Keepsakes*
OTHER: Toothpick flag

how to

Create the background for the right-hand page, smear a piece of cardstock with ink to give the look of camouflage. Then cut pieces of screen into various sizes and use them like colorblocks over the inked cardstock. Many of the edges are folded under and the blocks are overlapped to create interesting textures. Most of the blocks are attached with glue under the photo. Other blocks are secured with brads and eyelets.

Julie embossed a toothpick flag with clear embossing enamel. She also heat embossed over the metal tag after it was stamped to keep it from smearing.

Armored Personnel Carrier
A lightly armored, highly mobile vehicle used for reconnaissance missions, combat support and Patrol missions.

"I put on the gear and couldn't believe how heavy it was. The tank was cramped inside." - John

"They were guarding the tanks with real big guns.

I felt like I was heading into battle." - Jackson

Returning from a trip to Disneyland, we stopped

Rendezvous

USA

Modeling paste, typically used to create 3-D forms or to repair ceramics, is now being touted as a perfect texture for paper art projects. While this pH-neutral medium requires practice and experimentation, the end results will greatly add to your creations. Check out the samples in this chapter to see how to use modeling paste on a frame, as a background for a quotation, or even as caulking on a lens. And you're not limited to a smooth white background either; this texture can be manipulated to have a particular design or color.

CREATING YOURSELF
BY HEIDI SWAPP

PAPER: Seven Gypsies
MODELING PASTE: Liquitex
WATERCOLORS: Peerless
FIBER: Rubba Dub Dub, Art Sanctum
STAMPING INK: Tsukineko
WALNUT INK: Postmodern Design
CEMENT STAMPS: Hobby Lobby
OTHER: Hemp cord & compass rubber stamp

how TO

Cut a 12" x 12" piece of cardstock in half by cutting a wave pattern. Turn one of the halves over, so it is opposite of the other. Arrange the pieces over your background piece of cardstock to make a negative space wave pattern. Spread modeling paste over the pattern and remove when it's still wet. Repeat, making each wave pattern a little different. Stamp desired quotation onto wet paste with cement stamps. Watercolor the paste and background, adding walnut ink to darken.

To help your journaling stand out more, decoupage over patterned paper, then journal on top, after it has dried.

how TO

Julie showcased some of her favorite love letters from her husband on this layout. To imitate the look, photocopy letters onto white cardstock. Julie warns, "They can't be scanned and printed with an inkjet because the wetness of the modeling paste will cause the ink to run." Next, cut, arrange, and glue the copies to a base piece of cardstock to create the background. For extra interest, attach a few pieces of screen. Using a palette knife, lightly spread a layer of modeling paste over the page to partially obscure the love letters. A dried rose was embedded into the wet paste for an extra accent. Julie's title is rubber stamped onto ribbon. To create the panel on the right page, wrap a piece of screen around lightweight mat board, then spread modeling paste over the top. Add pictures. Print the years using a small font. Cut them to fit inside the small studs and adhere under each photo.

Note: To make the envelope blend with the look of the modeling paste, lightly rub the envelope with a white ink pad. The original love letters are tucked safely inside the envelope.

LOVE LETTERS
BY JULIE TURNER

MODELING PASTE: Liquitex
SCREEN: Wireform, American Art Clay Co.
DRIED FLOWERS: Pressed Petals
SATIN RIBBON: Offray
SILK EMBROIDERY RIBBON: Bucilla
METAL LEAFING: USArtQuest
INK: Encore Ultimate Metallic, Tsukineko
LETTER STAMPS: Antique Alphabet, PSX Design
ENVELOPE: Memory Lane
TAG: Sunday International
COMPUTER FONT: CK Chemistry, "Fresh Fonts" CD, Creating Keepsakes
ADHESIVE: Duo Embellishing Adhesive, USArtQuest
CHARM: Stevie Fresquez
OTHER: Metal ring studs

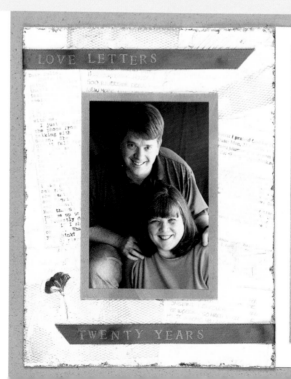

SHADOW BOX
BY DEBBIE CROUSE

MODELING PASTE: Liquitex
ADHESIVE: Glue Dots International
LETTER STAMPS: Carved in Stone Alphabet, Inkadinkado
PAINTER'S COMB: Royal and Langnickel
ACRYLIC PAINT: Antique White, Deco Art
PACKING TAPE: Scotch, 3M
SHADOW BOX: Pottery Barn
OTHER: Upholstery tack, fabric swatches, tassel cord, assorted found objects, and mat board

how to

Cut a frame from lightweight chipboard. Spread a thin layer of modeling paste over the frame and run a plastic fork across horizontally to create the design. Paint with acrylic paint when dry. To age the frame, blot with walnut ink. Affix the frame to your page with brads that have been painted with acrylic paint.

To make the ribbon photo corners, cut a ribbon to 3". Place the center of the ribbon over the corner on the front of your photo, wrap both ends around the back, and affix with tape.

To create the metal date plates, cut a rectangle piece from a metal sheet. Fold each side over 1/4". Unfold each side and cut off the corners at an angle. Cut a piece of paper to fit in the center and stamp the date. Put the paper on the metal and fold all sides again. Flatten with a bone folder. Heidi "finger painted" the metal with acrylic paint. Affix with adhesive dots. To attach the silk flower, remove the plastic center and set with an eyelet.

how TO

Cut mat board into four 3" squares. Cover the front of each square with modeling paste. Three of the squares were left smooth and Debbie ran a painter's comb through the other one to make the lines. The first square is wrapped with tape onto which an image has been transferred (see image transfer chapter). The "home" square was stamped with rubber stamps. On the third square, embed a large button in a puddle of modeling paste. Adorn the fourth square with fabric swatches and other ephemera. Use an upholstery tack to hold on the key. The fiber is wrapped around a piece of mat board that has been covered with modeling paste and cut into a square. When the 3" squares are dry, antique them with acrylic paint. Attach them to the shadow box with adhesive dots.

PAUL & SHER ANNIVERSARY
BY HEIDI SWAPP

VELLUM: Autumn Leaves
BRADS: Making Memories
ACRYLIC PAINT: Delta
SILK HYDRANGEAS: Michaels
COLORED PENCILS: Prismacolor
ADHESIVE: Glue Dots International
MODELING PASTE: Liquitex
OTHER: Aluminum sheet and silk flower

Modeling Paste

1 Julie suggests using Rives BFK paper as a base when working
   with modeling paste. She comments, "This artist's printmaking
   paper comes in big sheets, is about the weight of watercolor
   paper, and doesn't ripple when you apply the modeling paste."

2 Using a palette knife, spread a layer of modeling paste, the size
   of the stencil, over the paper. Make it as smooth as possible.

3 After the first layer is dry, position the stencil over the smooth
   layer and spread modeling paste over the top of the stencil to
   create the surface pattern. Lift the stencil and let the layer dry.

4 Color the entire surface with a light wash of watercolor.

5 When dry, lightly color the stems and leaves with a watercolor
   pencil. Using a small paintbrush dipped in water, paint over the
   penciled areas to give the look of watercolor.

6 When the watercolor is dry, antique with a light wash of walnut ink.

tips

- Trim your overall page down when using modeling paste
  so your page will fit easily into a page protector.

- Work quickly when manipulating modeling paste. And since
  modeling paste dries so quickly, clean as you go to make
  cleaning up easier!

- When using rubber stamps on the modeling paste, get
  them *slightly* damp first, so they don't stick to the paste.

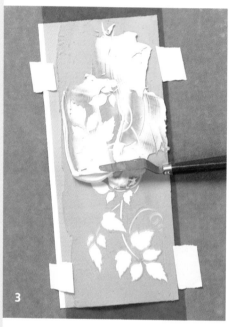

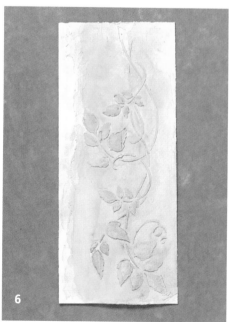

how TO

Cut chipboard to 7 1/2 " x 4 1/2". Score places to fold. (Debbie folded 1 1/2" up from the bottom and 2 1/2" down from the top.) Cover the front and back with paper. Let dry completely. Put ephemera underneath the convex lens and attach lens with modeling paste around the edges. When dry, antique the card with walnut ink, covering the paper, modeling paste area, and the tag on the inside. Set eyelets and tie closed.

This photo of my grandmother and her older sister has always been a favorite of mine. It is the only picture I have of her as a child and it was taken in Minnesota around 1897. How excited the girls must have been as they prepared and primped for their portrait. I love their hand-sewn dresses and long, flowing hair.

Eventually, Grandma cut her hair shorter. One Christmas she made dolls for each of her granddaughters, and used her own hair that she had saved to make hair on the dolls. My doll no longer exists, but I did save a lock of Grandma's hair.

Clara and Martha

SECRET MESSAGE
BY DEBBIE CROUSE

PAPER: Anna Griffin
HEMP CORD: Darice
ADHESIVE: PVA, Books by Hand
MODELING PASTE: Liquitex
WALNUT INK: Postmodern Design
TAG: American Tag
OPTICAL LENS: Manto Fev
EYELETS: Making Memories
OTHER: Fabric swatches and chipboard

SISTERS
BY JULIE TURNER

PRINTMAKING PAPER: Rives BFK
MODELING PASTE: Liquitex
WATERCOLORS: Windsor & Newton
WATERCOLOR PENCILS: Staedtler
WALNUT INK: Postmodern Design
EMBOSSING INK: Clear Emboss*it*, Ranger Industries
EMBOSSING ENAMEL: Ultra Thick Embossing Enamel, Suze Weinberg
SILK EMBROIDERY RIBBON: Bucilla
STENCIL: Buckingham Stencils, Inc.
COMPUTER FONT: Monet Regular, P22 Type Foundry
OTHER: Metal frame stud

What do you do with all of those bags you get when you go shopping or with pretty wrapping paper you carefully remove from a gift? Or what do you do with old maps or old books? Make them into paper art projects, of course! The artists truly create treasures by designing their own printed paper, incorporating printed memorabilia, and using scraps of accumulated printed papers on their creations.

ephemera (i fem′ə rə) n. minor, everyday documents… intended for one-time or short-term use, including postcards, broadsides and posters, baseball cards, tickets, bookmarks, photographs, etc.— from The Ephemera Society of America (www.ephemerasociety.org)

how to

Debbie started this project with a plan to use larger, unorthodox pieces of paper, such as wallpaper, maps, and store bags to make fun envelopes. As she began creating, she had to come up with a matching card and, of course, a portfolio to store the cards.

To make the envelopes, you need a template around which to tear the paper. You can buy ready-made templates or you can make your own. (To make your own template, take an envelope apart and use it as a pattern to create a template out of a heavy cardboard or mat board. Then cut out the template using a utility knife and a metal ruler.) Lay the template onto your paper and tear around the edges. Fold the flaps in and glue all of them down except the top flap. Envelope glue works well for the top flap. It can also be sealed later with glue or sealing wax.

For the cards, cut sturdy paper to fit the envelopes. Gather ephemera, fibers, string, ribbon, lace, squares of fabric, coordinating paper, and other notions. Line up your embellishments and machine stitch over the top.

how to

To give the map a worn look, wet, wrinkle, and iron it. Heidi cut a portion of the foam core away to hold an envelope that houses extra photos. She then placed a transparency over the opening to keep the envelope in place, yet allowing it to remain visible.

PLEASE WRITE
BY DEBBIE CROUSE

PRINTED PAPERS: Seven Gypsies and Bravissimo
ADHESIVE: PVA, Books by Hand; Lick and Stick (envelope adhesive), Green Sneakers, Inc.; Sealing wax, Alphabet Seals
ENVELOPE TEMPLATE: Kreate-a-lope, Green Sneakers, Inc.
UTILITY KNIFE: Olfa
ENVELOPE LABELS: Chronicle Books
OTHER: Pins, assorted ephemera, store bags, wallpaper, and scraps of fiber, string, ribbon, fabric, screen, and paper

SEDONA DAY TRIP
BY HEIDI SWAPP

FOAM CORE: Michaels
TRANSPARENCY: 3M
TOPOGRAPHICAL MAP: Mesa Blueprints
"Inspire" rubber stamp: Stampa Rosa
EYELETS: Making Memories

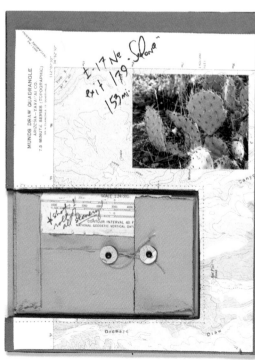

GLIMPSES OF MY YESTERDAYS

Patricia Anne Bushm[...]
BORN 10 February 1933
WHERE Idaho Falls, Bonne[...]
DIED
WHERE

Virginia Wagstaff
BORN 7 June 1904
WHERE Holladay, Salt Lake, Utah

I have been very blessed in my life that Virginia W. Bushman was my *grandmother*. Beyond family responsibilities, she was a teacher, family historian and *genealogist*. She loved her family members — past, present and future. Her life was filled with challenges, but her courage through those trials taught me many things.

Lessons I learned from Grandma

Her husband was killed by a drunk driver, leaving her with four children to care for. I never heard her speak a negative word about the driver.

I learned forgiveness.

Grandma was about 4'10". Her size never stopped her for a minute. She was a GIANT in all the important things in life.

I learned what matters most.

Grandma felt that she should make a family history book. She couldn't afford the cost of the printing so she bought a small press and learned how to print it herself.

I learned to believe in myself.

Although Grandma was widowed for 48 years, she talked about Grandpa all the time. I never met Grandpa, but I felt his love for his grandchildren through her. The glimmer in her eye never faded as she spoke of him.

I learned about lasting love.

BELIEVE

Silos Aikens Bushman
BORN 15 May 1893
WHERE Snowflake, Navajo,
WHEN MARRIED 3 June 1925
DIED 20 April 1950

how TO

Robin created the printed paper by enlarging some of the typed pages from her grandma's family history records and genealogy sheets. She also found her grandma's signature on an old card, so she enlarged it and copied it on top of the printed paper she created. Robin muses, "No printed scrapbooking paper I could have bought would illicit the same memories as seeing Grandma's signature and typing from her old typewriter."

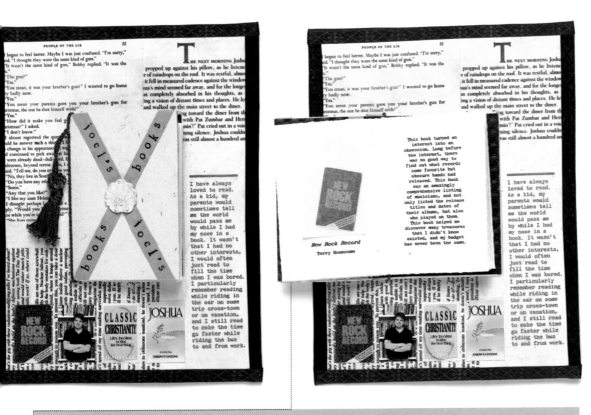

VIRGINIA W. BUSHMAN
BY ROBIN JOHNSON

LACE: Jo-Ann Fabrics
RUBBER STAMPS: "Believe," River City Rubber Works; Ruler, Limited Edition
CHARM: Embellish It, Boutique Trims
STAMPING INK: Brilliance, Tsukineko
COMPUTER FONTS: Typist and Textile
BUTTONS: From her grandma's old button box
OTHER: Metal piece and a glass flower marble

JOEL'S BOOKS
BY JULIE TURNER

PAPER: Bravissimo
ADHESIVE: Perfect Paper Adhesive (matte), USArtQuest
POWDERED PIGMENT: Pearl-Ex, Jacquard Products
LETTER STAMPS: Antique Alphabet, PSX Design
STAMPING INK: Crafter's Pigment Ink, Clearsnap; Shadow Ink, Hero Arts
COMPUTER FONT: Typewriter, P22 Type Foundry
TASSEL: JudiKins
OTHER: Dollhouse trim and glassine envelopes

how to

For the background, glue your journaling and pages torn from an extra copy of a favorite book onto cardstock. Julie adhered the paper with Perfect Paper Adhesive, and she rolled a brayer over the paper to eliminate air bubbles. When dry, brush the entire surface with another layer of Perfect Paper Adhesive. While that layer dries, pour some Perfect Paper Adhesive into a paper cup and stir in a small amount of gold Pearl-Ex. Brush this mixture over the entire surface to give the background paper an antiqued look. Finish your page by folding ribbon around the edges.

To make the book, fold 5" x 7" paper in half and tie a tassel around the middle to bind. The glassine envelopes were stained different colors by rubbing the entire surface with a dye ink pad.

decoupage

Decoupage, an old technique that comes from the French word *decouper* meaning to cut out, is used by mixed media artists to encase non-archival products on their works of art. Note how our artists employ this technique to affix printed paper and memorabilia to scrapbook pages and a frame with either Mod Podge or pH-neutral Perfect Paper Adhesive.

how to

With a utility knife and a metal ruler, cut two pieces of cardboard to 5 1/2" x 6 1/4". Cut a rectangular opening in the front piece. Cut a stand for your frame, using a store-bought frame as a pattern. Cut a transparency to the size of the photo you will be framing. Rubber stamp onto the transparency. Glue or sew the stand to the back cardboard piece. Position your photo and transparency between the two layers of cardboard and sew all the way around the outside edge of the frame.

To get the words on the front of the frame, iron kraft colored tissue paper onto freezer paper. Cut to 8 1/2" x 11". This enables you to run your tissue paper through your printer. Print the words onto tissue paper, tear around the words, and peel off the freezer paper. Decoupage the torn words to the frame with Diamond Glaze. When dry, apply another coat or two of the glaze. Tie the ribbon and hemp cord through the corrugation holes. Stitch on a swatch of fabric and affix the watch parts with E-6000. **Artist's tip:** Machine sewing through the cardboard was not a problem. Try it!

how TO

To incorporate ephemera into your layout, arrange it as a background by adhering it to your page with PVA and a brayer. Then decoupage the entire page by completely covering it with Perfect Paper (matte finish). To prevent the page from curling, temporarily affix your page to a piece of chipboard so it will dry flat. The article on the page was actually quite long, so Heidi clipped out the parts she wanted to remember and decoupaged them together so it looks like a seamless article. Add photographs. Use file label holders to hold captions for your photographs.

PRECIOUS TIME
BY DEBBIE CROUSE

FREEZER PAPER: Reynolds
RIBBON: Offray
EMBROIDERY FLOSS: DMC
ADHESIVE: E-6000, Eclectic Products; Diamond Glaze, JudiKins
RUBBER STAMPS: PSX Design (Antique Alphabet), Stampers Anonymous (clock face)
COMPUTER FONT: GF Halda Normal, Hootie, John Doe, and Linen Stroke, downloaded from the Internet; CK Constitution, "Fresh Fonts" CD, *Creating Keepsakes*
INK: StazOn, Tsukineko
UTILITY KNIFE: Olfa
METAL RULER: Pro Art
SAFETY PIN: Dritz
HEART: Mill Hill
HEMP CORD: Darice
WATCH PARTS: Manto Fev
OTHER: Kraft colored tissue paper, corrugated cardboard, and a crimp bead

NEW YORK TRIATHLON
BY HEIDI SWAPP

NEWSPAPER: *New York Times*
LABEL HOLDERS: Avery
ADHESIVE: PVA, Books by Hand; Perfect Paper Adhesive (matte), USArtQuest
PHOTO CORNERS: Canson
OTHER: "I Love NY" bumper sticker

FOUR GENERATIONS
BY HEIDI SWAPP

PATTERNED PAPER: K & Company
BEADS: Making Memories
ADHESIVE: Perfect Paper Adhesive, USArtQuest
OTHER: Buttons, corsage pin, braided trim, and chipboard

JEFFERSON MEMORIAL
BY JULIE TURNER

ADHESIVE: Perfect Paper Adhesive (glossy), USArtQuest
ACRYLIC PAINT: FolkArt, Plaid
EYELETS AND BRADS: Making Memories
FIBER: DMC
LABEL HOLDER: Anima Designs
GLASSINE ENVELOPES: Memory Lane
STAMPING INK: Ranger Industries
COMPUTER FONT: Dearest Script, P22 Type Foundry; Goudy Old Style, Word Pro
OTHER: Memorabilia from the Turner's trip

how to Half of the flower is decoupaged and the other half is not. To create the same look, cut portions of the flower out, petal by petal. Adhere the majority of the flower to the page and spread Perfect Paper over the top. When it is dry, attach a few more petals, completing the original design, but don't decoupage over the top petals. Roll back the edges of the exposed petals and leaves to give them more dimension.

how TO

After you have arranged your memorabilia on the layout, thoroughly glue it down with Perfect Paper Adhesive. Roll over it with a brayer to remove all the bubbles and to make the surface as smooth as possible. The text strip contains a quotation from Thomas Jefferson. When adding text such as this, it must be laser printed, photocopied, or written with a waterproof pen so it doesn't bleed when covered with Perfect Paper. The color of the map was very bright, so Julie toned it down by covering the entire surface of the page with a wash of thinned white acrylic paint. Wipe off the excess with a paper towel. When dry, decoupage the entire surface with a coat of Perfect Paper. Julie also stippled the decoupaged surface with brown dye ink. The brass brads and label holder also looked too bright, so Julie whitewashed them with acrylic paint.

To make room for more journaling, Julie attached a small accordion fold book to her layout. The cover of the book was made to line up with the part of the map it was covering, which in this case was the Jefferson Memorial.

13 crackle

Since the word "crackle" is an onomatopoeia, or a word that imitates the sound it represents, just saying the word sounds like texture moving over your lips. And when you use crackle on your creations, you instantly add texture and pizzazz. Check out how the artists crackle their projects with either embossing enamel or a pH-neutral crackle medium and paint, creating an illusion of depth and antiquity.

how to

To obtain a crackled look in random places on your layout, you'll need canvas paper, which is available at a craft or art supply store. Paint a base color onto the canvas paper with acrylic paint. Allow to dry. Paint crackle medium generously over the spots you want to crackle and allow to dry. Paint a topcoat onto the entire canvas with full strength acrylic paint. Heidi found that diluted paint does not crackle well. Allow to dry and cracks will appear. Heidi also randomly brushed on more of her base color paint to add more texture. Paint the foam stamp with ivory paint and stamp portions onto the paper. Then apply green paint to the stamp and stamp again, overlapping the ivory image. The right side of the layout is foam core, which allows for the shell necklace and coins. You can do your lettering once the paint is dry, but use a pencil first! After your canvas is totally dry, cut it down to 8 1/2" x 11". (And if you were wondering, no, this picture is not of Heidi in a bikini!)

how TO

The crackle on this page was created by heat embossing two layers of clear embossing enamel over a subtle plaid-patterned paper. After embossing, put the paper in the freezer for a few minutes to make the surface easier to crack. Then bend the paper in different directions. Give the cracks an aged look by rubbing the entire surface with a brown dye ink pad. Wipe off the excess, leaving the ink only in the cracks.

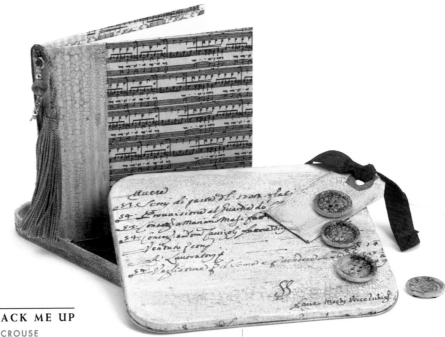

MOMENTS OF PERFECTION
BY HEIDI SWAPP

CANVAS PAPER: Strathmore
ACRYLIC PAINT: FolkArt, Plaid
CRACKLE MEDIUM: FolkArt Crackle Medium, Plaid
FLEUR DE LEIS FOAM STAMP: Stamp Décor, Plaid
MESH PAPER: Magenta
FOAM CORE: Office Max
LETTERING: Artist's own handwriting

HUMPHREYS PEAK
BY JULIE TURNER

PAPER: Patchwork Papers
EMBOSSING INK: Clear Emboss*it*, Ranger Industries
STAMPING INK: Sienna, Ancient Page, Clearsnap
EMBOSSING ENAMEL: Ultra Thick Embossing Enamel, Suze Weinberg
SNAPS: Making Memories
COMPASS: Manto Fev
MAP: Mesa Blueprints

IVY AND CAT
BY JULIE TURNER

PAPER: Rives BFK
ACRYLIC PAINT: FolkArt, Plaid
CRACKLE MEDIUM: FolkArt Crackle Medium, Plaid
CANVAS: Jo-Ann Fabrics
GESSO: Liquitex
STAMPING INK: ColorBox Fluid Chalk, Clearsnap
EYELETS: Coffee Break Designs
COMPUTER FONT: CK Extra, "Fresh Fonts" CD, *Creating Keepsakes*

YOU CRACK ME UP
BY DEBBIE CROUSE

PRINTED PAPERS: Renaissance, Seven Gypsies, and Liz King
ADHESIVE: PVA, Books by Hand
TOOLS: X-Acto knife
ADHESIVE: Mod Podge Gloss, Plaid
CRACKLE MEDIUM: FolkArt Eggshell Crackle Step 1 and Step 2, Plaid
WALNUT INK: Postmodern Designs
TAG: Avery
TASSEL: India House
SPRING AND BEADS: Ink It!
METAL CD TIN: Stampa Rosa
OTHER: Chipboard, magnet strips, and bias tape

how to

Cover your mini-book as shown in the aging chapter. For a decorative binding, attach a contrasting strip of paper, folded in half. Crackle the spine according to the directions below, then bind with a tassel and cord.

Cover the lid of a tin with paper using PVA. Clip around the corners of the paper, so they will lay flat. Trim the paper next to the ridge of the tin with an X-Acto knife. Apply a coat of decoupage medium over the paper and book spine. If you want your book and tin crackled, it is important to use the glossy decoupage medium. When dry, apply the crackle medium as directed. Debbie found it important when applying step two of the crackle medium, to apply a thick coat and to brush it as little as possible. When dry and when you can see the crackle (don't rush the drying time!), work walnut ink into the cracks with your finger. Debbie also crackled and inked the tag and buttons. The buttons are attached with magnet strips.

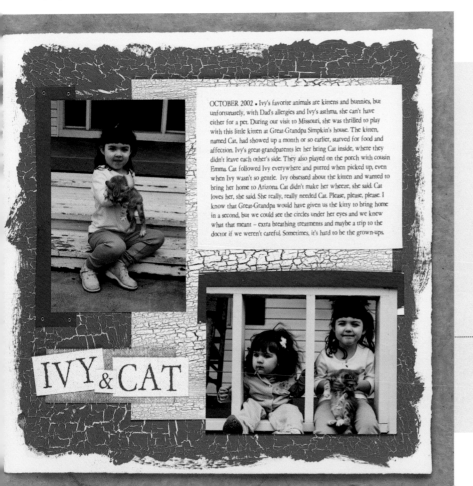

OCTOBER 2002 • Ivy's favorite animals are kittens and bunnies, but unfortunately, with Dad's allergies and Ivy's asthma, she can't have either for a pet. During our visit to Missouri, she was thrilled to play with this little kitten at Great-Grandpa Simpkin's house. The kitten, named Cat, had showed up a month or so earlier, starved for food and affection. Ivy's great-grandparents let her bring Cat inside, where they didn't leave each other's side. They also played on the porch with cousin Emma. Cat followed Ivy everywhere and purred when picked up, even when Ivy wasn't so gentle. Ivy obsessed about the kitten and wanted to bring her home to Arizona. Cat didn't make her wheeze, she said. Cat loves her, she said. She really, really needed Cat. Please, please, please. I know that Great-Grandpa would have given us the kitty to bring home in a second, but we could see the circles under her eyes and we knew what that meant – extra breathing treatments and maybe a trip to the doctor if we weren't careful. Sometimes, it's hard to be the grown-ups.

IVY & CAT

how TO

To achieve the white crackly look, paint a coat of FolkArt Crackle Medium over a piece of dark gray cardstock. When dry, paint with a coat of white acrylic craft paint. The layer of crackle medium underneath will make the white topcoat crackle as it dries.

To create the red crackle, paint the background paper with a base coat of white acrylic craft paint. Julie prefers using Rives BFK paper for this type of project to prevent rippling. When dry, paint with a layer of FolkArt Crackle Medium. The thicker the coat of crackle, the larger the cracks will be. When the crackle layer has dried, paint on a topcoat, such as the red Julie used on this layout.

aging&walnut ink

Finally! Here is one thing in your life you actually want to look aged and old. The artists explore several products that can add years to your projects: sandpaper (try several grits), steel wool, ink pads, Rub-Ons, paint, powdered pigment, and walnut ink. They also age their projects by adding ephemera, by bending and rolling corners, and peeling back layers of paper. So put away the anti-aging creams and get out your aging toolbox to add a vintage look to your creations!

Aging Cardstock how to

This is a quick technique that adds depth and interest to background papers.

1 Completely immerse cardstock in water.

2 Wad into a ball and squeeze out excess water.

3 Carefully open and smooth out.

4 Allow to dry in sunlight for a more rugged look.

5 Or iron the paper on the cotton setting. Ironing not only smoothes out wrinkles, but it also quickly dries the paper.

how to

This journal comes with "naked" covers so you can do whatever you want to create your own unique look. Debbie wanted a vintage look, so she used an old postcard, ticket stubs, music from an old hymnal, and pages from a 1931 magazine. She slipped the front and back covers out of the binding and used PVA glue to attach the ephemera. You may choose to decoupage the covers to protect the fragile papers. The book corners slip on and the latch was attached with brads. The unique binding allows pages to turn from alternating sides.

BEFORE

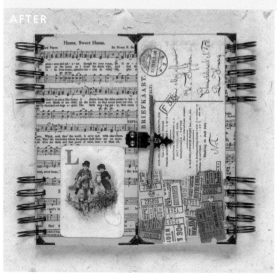

AFTER

OLD DUFFER

BY DEBBIE CROUSE

ADHESIVE: PVA, Books by Hand
JOURNAL AND METAL CORNERS: Seven Gypsies
LATCH: Schlage
BRADS: Art Brads
OTHER: Old music, postcards, ticket stubs, and an old magazine

Book Covering
how to

1. Cut chipboard to size and score where you want the folds. Cut the paper that will be on the outside 1" larger on all sides of the chipboard. Pre-fold the outside paper to line up with the folds in the chipboard.

2. Cover the outside of the chipboard with PVA and place paper on the chipboard, lining up the folds/score lines.

3. Use a brayer to ensure the paper is completely adhered.

4. To get a mitered corner, cut paper down to the chipboard on a 45° angle at each corner.

5. Cover outside edges with PVA and fold over. Again, use a brayer.

6. Measure and cut the inside paper 1/8" - 1/4" smaller than the chipboard to reveal the outside paper. Evenly paint PVA to the back of the inside paper and use a brayer to adhere it to the inside. Run the side of the bone folder into the folds to ensure the paper is completely adhered to the chipboard and to help your book to fold.

7. Age and distress to finish.

Original paper:
This is what the paper looked like before any of the aging techniques.

Stippled with Brown Dye Ink:
Using a special stipple brush, lightly stipple the surface with brown ink.

Lumiere:
Brush with a coat of Lumiere, an iridescent paint.

Pearl-Ex mixed with Perfect Paper Adhesive:
Mix a small amount of gold Pearl-Ex with Perfect Paper Adhesive to make a paint. Paint over the surface of the paper. As the paint is drying, you can dry brush a little more powder across the surface for added effect.

Plaid Antiquing Medium:
Brush or sponge the brown antiquing medium over the surface of the paper and gently wipe off any excess. Use full-strength for a very dark brown or water it down for a lighter color.

White Acrylic Paint:
Slightly water down white acrylic craft paint and brush it over the surface of the paper. Gently wipe the excess off with a paper towel.

walnut ink

You'll literally go nuts for these ideas! Walnut ink, which is made from old, shriveled walnuts and which comes in crystal form, can be used to write with, to mute a background design, or to age paper. After you make the ink by mixing the crystals with water according to the recipe on the container, store the prepared ink in an airtight container. It'll keep for at least six months.

In this chapter, the artists illustrate creative ways to use and apply the ink. Heidi hand-lettered on her layout with a calligraphy nib, a detail paintbrush, and highly concentrated walnut ink. Julie simply brushed the walnut ink over the top of her background page. And Deb shook tags in a plastic bag, covering them with the ink. Experiment with this fun product; you'll love the results!

how to

Debbie used three envelopes that were lying around without cards. Paint the envelopes with walnut ink. Cut a heavy piece of cardboard and slip it inside one of the envelopes to give them some bulk. Adhere small elements to the top envelope. Cut a transparency to size and embellish with rubber stamps. Bundle them together with string. Slip a message under the string in back.

how to

Adhere fabric to your page with fusible web. Write the word "individual" with walnut ink and a detail paintbrush, then journal over the top with walnut ink and a calligraphy nib. With a paper towel, wash walnut ink over the top of a strip of paper and over the letter "J." When dry, write additional words on the letter "J." On this layout, Heidi wrote the boys' names: Scott and Andy.

LETTERS
BY DEBBIE CROUSE

TRANSPARENCIES: 3M
BIAS TAPE AND CANVAS: Jo-Ann Fabrics
ADHESIVE: Zig 2-Way Glue
RUBBER STAMPS: Savvy Stamps ("thank you"), Office Max (date stamp)
STAMPING INK: StazOn, Tsukineko
TAG: American Tag
FERN: Nature's Pressed
WALNUT INK: Postmodern Design
OTHER: Envelopes and string

OPPOSITES ATTRACT
BY HEIDI SWAPP

BUTTONS: Making Memories
WALNUT INK: Postmodern Design
OTHER: Fabric, watercolor paper, calligraphy nib, and a detail paintbrush

The background paper started out as a piece of plain white cardstock. To get the striped look, drag an ink pad across your paper and brush over the top with walnut ink. **Note:** Since the archival nature of walnut ink is unknown, Julie backed her photos with an acid-free buffered paper.

7/4/2002 • After a day of gliding across the water with the wind in their sails, Jason and Jeanette dropped anchor in Coronado Bay to take in the fireworks over San Diego. Hundreds of boats, many with patriotic decorations, filled the waters. Everyone was in a festive mood, enjoying and celebrating the freedoms we hold dear.

FREEDOM

BY JULIE TURNER

PRINTMAKING PAPER: Rives BFK
LETTER STAMPS: Vintage Alphabet, Hero Arts
STAMPING INK: Crafter's Pigment Ink, Clearsnap
WALNUT INK: Postmodern Design
EYELETS AND SNAPS: Making Memories
HEMP CORD: Darice
TAGS: American Tag
TRANSPARENCY: 3M
COMPUTER FONT: Typewriter, P22 Type Foundry
OTHER: Cotton-twill tape and a dog tag

TAGS

BY DEBBIE CROUSE

WALNUT INK: Postmodern Design
HEMP CORD: Darice
RUBBER STAMPS: Antique Alphabet, PSX Design; Printer's Lower Case, Hero Arts; Seal stamp, Hampton Arts
STAMPING INK: Sepia, Archival Ink, Ranger Industries
TAGS: Avery
OTHER: Sealing wax, crimp bead, and a Ziploc bag

1 Tags before applying walnut ink.

2 Lightly coat the tags with walnut ink and bundle them together with twine and sealing wax.

3 Lightly coat the tags with walnut ink, then rubber stamp.

4 Crinkle the tags, then coat heavily with walnut ink. Debbie "doubled dipped" the tags to get a darker color.

how TO

Slightly dilute a little walnut ink in a Ziploc bag according to the manufacturer's directions. Put the tags in the bag and shake, making sure they are well coated. To get more color in the folds, crinkle the tags before putting them in the Ziploc. If you want a lighter color, get them in and out of the bag quickly. Debbie learned this technique from Donna Smylie whose husband kept throwing away her bowl of ink when she left it out. To remedy the situation, Donna put the ink in a Ziploc bag and found it was much quicker and much cleaner to apply. These tags can be used on anything: cards, scrapbook pages, art journals, and more.

15 acrylic paint

You've probably used acrylic paint on wood projects and for stenciling, but have you used it on scrapbook pages or cards? This inexpensive, pH-neutral product, which comes in almost every color imaginable, can help you create customized backgrounds, images, or journaling blocks. So pull out your painting supplies and use them to create colorful art projects.

how to

Brush paint onto your child's hands and feet with a sponge brush and "stamp" onto cardstock.

QUINCY TOES

BY HEIDI SWAPP

EMBOSSED PAPER: Black Ink
PRINTED PAPER: Autumn Leaves
RIBBON: Offray
STUDS: Diane Ribbon and Notion Co.
ACRYLIC PAINT: Delta

how to

Tear a large watercolor sheet to size using a straight edge. With low-tack tape, tape off the areas you wish to paint. Dilute paint as needed. (Heidi added just a touch of water.) Paint inside the taped area for a customized background. Using clear embossing enamel, heat emboss the printed paper on the pocket to make the paper appear slightly translucent. Tie an old key to the hidden tag with fibers. For instructions on writing with walnut ink, refer to the walnut ink chapter.

LOVE

BY HEIDI SWAPP

PRINTED PAPER: Renaissance Prints
ACRYLIC PAINT: Delta
METAL LETTERS: Making Memories
FIBERS: Adornaments, K1C2
CHARM: Embellish it!
WALNUT INK: Postmodern Design
EMBOSSING ENAMEL: Ultra Thick Embossing Enamel, Suze Weinberg
EMBOSSING INK: Clear Emboss*it*, Ranger Industries
TAG: American Tag
BRADS: Lost Art, American Tag
OTHER: Calligraphy nib and watercolor paper

how TO

Cut chipboard to 4 1/2" x 10". Cover the front and back of the chipboard with paper using the method in the aging chapter. Your finished cover will be a 4 1/2" square. Stamp your design onto the cover using acrylic paint as your ink. Add ephemera, then wash the entire cover with walnut ink. Decoupage the items that will be under the glass slide, then adhere the slide with Diamond Glaze. Attach the clasp and jewelry finding with brads.

For the inside, fold paper along the lines as shown. Put glue on both sides of the house shape and sandwich it between the chipboard card, putting the point of the "house" towards the fold. Let dry. When you open the card, the paper will unfold. Swish acrylic paint over the patterned paper to create a writing surface.

folding directions:

Folding the paper for the inside of the card looks complicated, but it's actually only 5 steps! This surprise foldout works great in a card or as a hidden journal block on a page. Start with an 8 1/2" square.

1   Fold the square corner to corner, creating an "X" with the fold lines.

2   Fold the square in half. Unfold.

3   Fold both sides to the centerline. Unfold.

4   Turn the paper one turn to the left and fold the other two sides to the center. Unfold.

5   Fold the square in half again, then (with the fold at the top) push the top two sides in towards the middle so they meet. Your paper will look like a triangle. Now push the four points in towards the middle. Your finished product should look similar to the shape of a house.

Note: Debbie reinforced the center point folds with tape to keep them from tearing.

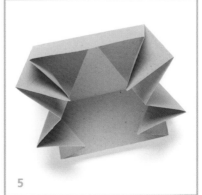

FOLD UP

BY DEBBIE CROUSE

PRINTED PAPER: Anna Griffin
RICK-RACK: Jo-Ann Fabrics
ACRYLIC PAINT: Delta
ADHESIVE: Perfect Paper Adhesive, USArtQuest; Diamond Glaze, JudiKins
FLEUR DE LEIS FOAM STAMP: Stamp Décor, Plaid
WALNUT INK: Postmodern Design
TAG: American Tag
GLASS SLIDE: Manto Fev
BRADS: American Pin & Fastener and Art Brads
METAL CLASP: Michaels (taken from a little wooden box)
OTHER: Chipboard

Walt Disney once commented, "It's kind of fun to do the impossible." Did you ever think it was possible to put words on stone or to put pictures on packing tape? With image transfer techniques, these extreme ideas can now be a reality. If an image isn't on a medium you can use for your projects, transfer the image to a medium that will work. Image transfer products also allow you to apply images to various textures. For example, Heidi was able to transfer a title and a photo to chipboard, creating a customized page embellishment ("San Francisco"). Have fun doing what many people would consider impossible!

JOY

BY ROBIN JOHNSON

WATERCOLOR PENCILS: Derwent
WATER PEN: Kuretake
COLORLESS BLENDER: Eberhard Faber
PEN: Zig Writer
METAL SHAPES AND FIBERS: Making Memories
SQUARE LETTERS: Global Solutions
LETTERING: Artist's own handwriting

how to

Make a color copy of your photo. Turn the picture face down onto a piece of cardstock. Using a colorless blender pen, color over the area of the picture you want transferred. Repeat three or four times so the paper is saturated. Carefully peel the paper back to see if the image has transferred. If it has not, replace the paper and continue on.

Instead of using watercolors for your letters, Robin suggests a quicker solution: watercolor pencils and a water pen. Fill in your letters with the pencil, then brush over them with a water pen to smooth and blend.

how to

The stone embellishments are thinly cut stone tile purchased from Home Depot. Julie didn't want them to be raised on the page, so she used foam core to make small shadow boxes. The words were added to the rocks with Lazertran, an image transfer material that works like a decal. Photocopy any image or word onto the Lazertran, and after soaking the paper in water, adhere the decal to almost any surface, including paper, fabric, glass, tile, and stone. The Lazertran was a little shinier than the stone, so to make the edges blend smoothly into the stone, Julie covered the entire surface with a thin coat of matte Mod Podge.

LEARN. OBSERVE. ENJOY.

BY JULIE TURNER

FOAM CORE: Office Max
ROCK PEBBLES AND FRAME: Jeffrey Court, Inc.
TRANSFER PAPER: Lazertran
COMPUTER FONT: CK Gutenberg, "Fresh Fonts" CD, *Creating Keepsakes*; Insectile, P22 Type Foundry
EMBOSSING INK: Clear Embossit, Ranger Industries
EMBOSSING ENAMEL: Ultra Thick Embossing Enamel, Suze Weinberg
ADHESIVE: Mod Podge, Plaid
OTHER: Vellum

You can use magazines, old books, or photocopies of images to make these transfers. Put the packing tape sticky side down over the image you want to copy. Turn it over so the picture is on the top and rub over the entire surface to make sure it is well adhered to the tape. Then put it under water and let it soak for a minute or two. Gently rub off the paper from the back, leaving just the ink from the image. Allow transfer to dry before attaching it to your project. No tape or other adhesive was used because the transfer was still sticky. Debbie had fun putting the transfer onto vellum tags because you can still see though all the layers.

how to

Print a reverse image of your title and photo onto the transfer paper. Following the package directions, iron it onto chipboard. Distress the chipboard by bending it, peeling back a few layers, and using Rub-Ons and chalk. Attach the chipboard to the page by punching holes in the chipboard and background paper and securing it with hemp.

Lettering tip: To continue the rustic look, dilute 1 teaspoon of bleach in 1/2 cup of water and use a calligraphy dip pen to write your journaling.

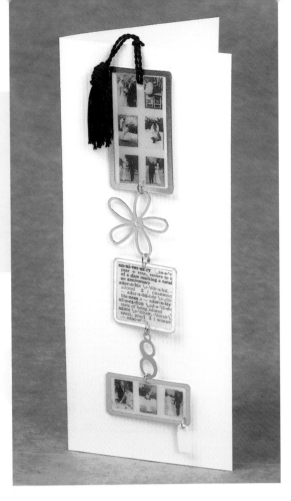

PACKING TAPE IMAGE TRANSFER
BY DEBBIE CROUSE

CLEAR PACKING TAPE: 3M
VELLUM TAGS, METAL FLOWER, AND NUMBER: Making Memories
TAG: Avery
OTHER: Jump rings and tassel

SAN FRANCISCO
BY HEIDI SWAPP

COMPASS STAMP: Uptown Design
RUB-ONS: Craf-T Products
PHOTO CORNERS: Canson
TRANSFER PAPER: Transfer Paper for Inkjet/Bubble Jet Printers, Transfer Magic
LETTERING: Artist's own handwriting
OTHER: Chipboard, bleach, calligraphy pen, and hemp cord

17 embossing

An elevated surface adds texture to almost anything. So embossing, which forms a raised surface, can be a simple way to add more feeling and appeal to your projects. Use dry or heat embossing to enhance your layouts or cards to produce a product that will tempt one to touch its surface.

how to

Cut cardstock into strips and determine their placement on your page. Rubber stamp words onto the strips with different styles of letters. Remove the strips from the base cardstock. Dab clear embossing ink all over the strips, cover with clear embossing enamel, and heat emboss. Reposition and adhere them to your page.

FRESH
BY HEIDI SWAPP

BUTTONS: Making Memories
EMBOSSING ENAMEL: Ultra Thick Embossing Enamel, Suze Weinberg
EMBOSSING ENAMEL: Clear Emboss*it*, Ranger Industries
LETTER STAMPS: Antique Alphabet, PSX Design
STAMPING INK: Ancient Page, Clearsnap
OTHER: Braided trim

how TO

The embossed strips are made with an old label maker that traditionally uses sticky-backed plastic strips. Cut cardstock strips 3/8" to 1/2" wide and the length of the paper. Practice with it a little, as some cardstock works better than others. Debbie found that cardstock with a slight texture such as linen works better than smooth paper. The label maker Debbie used allowed her to tuck the end of the strip into the machine. For the body of the card, cut 8 1/2" x 11" cardstock in half lengthwise. The end flap is 1 3/8" and the body is 4" long when folded. Score and fold, creating a matchbook. Sew or glue the embossed strips to the card under the end flap. Debbie also sewed printed paper over the end flap. Eyelets on both sides of the card hold the flap and name strip down. Embellish with ribbon and beads. "To grandma" is attached with a split ring. To close, tuck the right flap into the end flap like a matchbook.

ELIZA
BY DEBBIE CROUSE

PRINTED PAPER: Anna Griffin
RIBBON: May Arts
ADHESIVE: HERMAfix
COMPUTER FONT: Cezanne, P22 Type Foundry
LABEL MAKER: Rotex
OTHER: Beads and a split ring

PEACEFUL SLUMBER

BY JULIE TURNER

PAPER: K & Company

FABRIC: Jo-Ann Fabrics

STAMPING INK: VersaColor, Tsukineko

EMBOSSING ENAMEL: Clear Emboss*it*, Ranger Industries

TRANSPARENCY: 3M (for laser printer)

DRIED FOWERS: Pressed Petals

FRAME: Memory Lane

BEADS: Westrim

CHARMS: Paper Parachute

SILK EMBROIDERY RIBBON: Bucilla, Plaid

PHOTO TAPE: 3L

COMPUTER FONT: CK Elegant, "Fresh Fonts" CD, *Creating Keepsakes*

MY FOREIGN SKY

BY ROBIN JOHNSON

PHOTOGRAPHER: Dave Tevis

VELLUM: Autumn Leaves

TEXTURED PAPER AND LEAVES: Black Ink

STENCIL: Wordsworth

COMPUTER FONTS: Monotype Corsiva, Felicia Plain, Copperplate Gothic, and Edwardian Script

SPIRAL PAPER CLIPS: Clipiola

LETTER STAMPS: PSX Design and PrintWorks

EMBOSSING PEN: Zig Emboss

EMBOSSING ENAMEL: Ultra Thick Embossing Enamel, Suze Weinberg

SHEER BAG: It's a Keeper

how TO

Lightly tack a dried flower to a piece of transparency with a dab of embossing ink. Then cover the entire surface, including the flower, with a light coat of embossing ink. Sprinkle with clear embossing enamel and heat emboss. Use transparency film made for laser printers so it will not melt. In this example, the embossed squares are stitched on.

This layout consists of three layers—printed paper, mat board, and cardstock—held together with photo tape. Cut square openings into the printed paper. Cut corresponding holes in the mat board. The mat board will create a shadowbox effect with a little less bulk than if you used foam core. The cardstock layer on the bottom has embossed areas that will show through as backgrounds for the squares. Julie also embossed the photo mat.

how to

The title ("Crissy") was embossed using a letter stencil and an embossing pen. Fill in the letters through the stencil. Sprinkle with embossing enamel and heat set. Robin used letter stamps and embossing enamel to emboss the other letters. To age your type as Robin did on the large journaling block, print out your text. Using white acrylic paint and a stencil brush, dry brush over the letters. Photocopy the text, reducing it 25%. Then take the reduced copy and enlarge it 400%. Reducing then enlarging the text creates the distorted and aged look.

The sheer bag holds a tiny lock of hair.

18 rubbings

Capture the textures you see outdoors or that are meaningful to you by creating rubbings. These implied textures give an illusion of depth when in reality the surface is smooth. Known as one of the oldest techniques in printmaking, rubbings are a simple and inexpensive way to add texture to your page.

how to

Lay a frame under cardstock. Rub crayons over the patterned area to obtain the design. Repeat on your background paper and on the journaling block.

To create the "slide-ins" for your photos and journaling blocks, place your page elements on paper and trace around them with a pencil. Remove the elements and lightly sketch where you want the slits to cross over your element. Using an X-Acto knife and a self-healing mat, cut along the lines that will create the crossover slits. Heidi cut them about 1/8" longer on each end to allow for the element to slide easily into the background paper.

how to

Add variety to your rubbings by using different colors of tissue paper and crayons.

CAM & LARANE
BY HEIDI SWAPP

CRAYONS: Crayola
LABEL HOLDER: woodworker.com
OTHER: Metal plate

JACKSON'S WORLD
BY JULIE TURNER

TISSUE PAPER: Hallmark
ARCHIVAL MIST: Preservation Technologies
CRAYON: Crayola
METAL: American Art Clay Co.
METAL STAMPS: Pittsburgh
STAMPING INK: Crafter's Pigment Ink, Clearsnap
TAGS AND METAL RING: American Tag
COMPUTER FONT: CK Extra, "Fresh Fonts" CD, *Creating Keepsakes*
EYELETS AND SNAPS: Making Memories
OTHER: Denim and a GAP tag

how TO

Debbie's son, Skyler, needed a way to ask his date to Homecoming, so they created rubbings from places around the school campus. They also wrote clues to go with each rubbing. The rubbing and its clue were placed in a packet. The final rubbing was from the bottom of Skyler's shoe, and the last clue led his date to the football game, where she had to find the boy wearing the shoe that matched the rubbing. Debbie and Skyler had a lot of fun and found it fairly easy to find places to do the rubbings. For their supplies, they used rice paper and a brown crayon. Some of the things you may want to take a rubbing of are a locker number plate (include the combination and hide the next clue in the locker), a school or building sign, or an engraved plaque.

For the packets, create a portfolio-type card by folding the paper up from the bottom, forming a pocket. Attach eyelets on each side. Lace the metal numbers on the cord and tie closed. Attach your clues to tags with a tiny straight pin and insert them into the pockets. (By the way, Skyler's date said yes!)

CLUE
BY DEBBIE CROUSE

RICE PAPER: Target Corp.
HEMP CORD: Darice
LETTER AND NUMBER STAMPS: Handprint, Turtle Press
COMPUTER FONT: CK Constitution, "Fresh Fonts" CD, *Creating Keepsakes*
STAMPING INK: Memories and Ranger Industries
EYELETS AND METAL NUMBERS: Making Memories
TAGS: Avery
BRADS: American Tag
CRAYONS: Crayola

EL CAMINO
BY HEIDI SWAPP

SNAPS: Dritz
PHOTO HOLDERS: Cleerline Products
CRAYONS: Crayola
COMPUTER FONT: John Doe, downloaded from the Internet
LETTER STAMPS: Antique Alphabet, PSX Design
ADHESIVE: Mod Podge, Plaid
METALLIC RUB-ONS: Craf-T Products
OTHER: Lightweight chipboard and a brown paper bag

how to

Lay cardstock on the metal letters of a car. Rub first in black, then in brown for more depth and interest. For the journaling block, print your text on two different colors of cardstock. Cut out the key words you wish to highlight from one color, then place them over the same spot on the other color of cardstock.

To make the folding mini-book inspired by an 80's-style Velcro wallet, cover lightweight chipboard with a brown paper bag that has been wet, crinkled, and ironed. Cover with Mod Podge to harden. Set two snaps to hold it closed. The 4" x 6" photo holders came three per page, so Heidi just cut off the bottom half that had two slots. She then sewed two "pages" of photo holders into the book to accommodate eight photos. To secure the book to your page, cut a slit in your background paper that is as long as your book and 1/4" wide. The flap of the book comes through the slit from the back and the rest wraps around the layout. You will also need to cut a slit in the sheet protector to allow the back of the book to fold to the front. Since the book wraps around one side of the page, it doesn't need to be glued on.

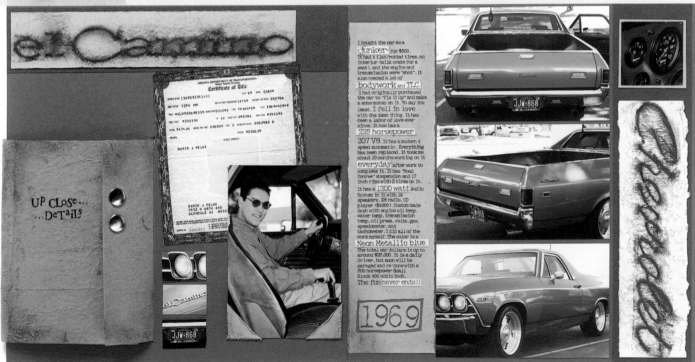

anything goes

Even with all of these fun and innovative textures, sometimes it's enjoyable to create a page just for fun, when "anything goes!" Let the artists' creativity inspire you as you look for new ideas and techniques you can apply to your projects.

how to Painting on canvas is a simple way to make a custom-colored, textured background for a special photo. Using a brush, cover a piece of canvas with acrylic gesso. Gesso, which is used by painters to prime their canvases, can be purchased in the paint department of craft stores. When dry, use acrylic paint to create a design that coordinates with your photos. To create the journaling block, Julie painted a piece of canvas with gesso, taped it to a sheet of printer paper, and ran it through her inkjet printer.

BATHING BEAUTY
BY JULIE TURNER

CANVAS: Jo-Ann Fabrics
ACRYLIC GESSO: Liquitex
ACRYLIC PAINT: FolkArt, Plaid
BUTTONS: Making Memories
FIBER: DMC
COMPUTER FONT: CK Sassy, "Fresh Fonts" CD,
Creating Keepsakes

how TO The rectangles are from a sheet of perforated business cards. The coated paper helped the ink color to stay bright. After rubbing an ink pad across the rectangles, cover them with embossing enamel, and heat emboss to create the water-like crystals. Rub the mesh with ink and adhere to the rectangles. Robin created the title and fish image by color copying the cover of one of her family's favorite books: *Rainbow Fish*.

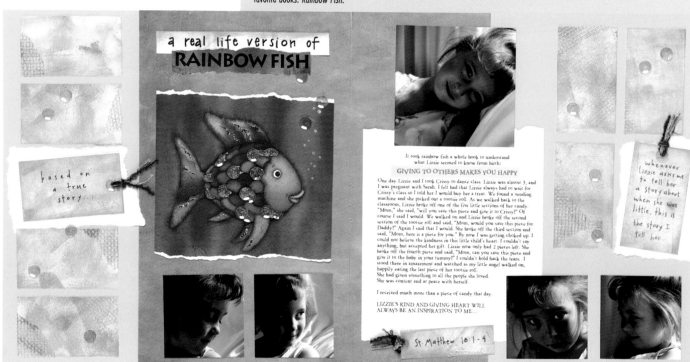

how TO To tie this layout together, Heidi cut slits in the base cardstock (tan) to overlap the green background papers. Mark the width you would like your slits so they will accommodate the items you will be sliding through. Cut the straight lines with a paper trimmer and cut the curves with an X-Acto knife. Slip the background papers and photos through the cutouts. Set eyelets to hold in place. The same concept is used for the journaling block in the upper left corner. Heidi cut it out from the base cardstock and overlapped it to the front.

A GIVING HEART

BY ROBIN JOHNSON

MESH: Michaels
FIBERS: Ink It!
STAMPING INK: Brilliance, Tsukineko
SEQUINS: Cousin Corp.
EMBOSSING ENAMEL: Ultra Thick Embossing Enamel, Suze Weinberg
ADHESIVE: Glue Dots International
COMPUTER FONT: Garamouche, P22 Type Foundry

BEACH BUDS

BY HEIDI SWAPP

VELLUM: Paper Adventures
SNAPS: Making Memories
COLORED PENCILS: Prismacolor
OTHER: Textured paper

REMEMBER WHEN BAGS

BY DEBBIE CROUSE

TRANSFER MEDIUM: Picture This, Plaid
MUSLIN BAGS: Memory Lane
TAGS: Avery
OTHER: Cord

how TO Make photocopies (dry toner) of your photos and cut them out. Wrap a piece of cardboard with waxed paper and insert it into the bag. Place the bag face up on another piece of waxed paper. Brush a thick coat of transfer medium onto the printed side of your photocopy. Place the copy onto the bag, photo side down. Cover with a paper towel. Using the transfer medium bottle, lightly roll over the entire copy. Remove the paper towel. Press around the outside edges with your finger. Let dry for 24 hours. When dry, saturate the copy with a wet sponge and let it set for 2 minutes. Gently rub off all the paper covering the photo. Read the directions on the bottle for more detailed instructions.

Artist's note: Debbie created these keepsake bags to house ornaments for her family's annual ornament exchange. She thought those relatives receiving ornaments would enjoy seeing their grandpa or great-grandpa in a little different light. These bags are inexpensive, and it's easy to add the transfer.

FINAL
Word

What you have seen in these pages only scratches the surface of possibilities for these products and techniques. **Experimentation** will be the key to your success and discovery. It is fun to keep your experimentations, see your progress, and learn from past discoveries and failures! I do my experimentations in an altered book. To make an altered book, choose a book you don't care about or purchase an old book from a thrift store. You may want to recover your book with paper or fabric or even paint or stain the existing cover. There are **limitless** ways to work in an altered book. And there are no rules; just **go crazy!** I used simple bookbinding techniques as seen in the aging chapter to recover the book with cross-stitch linen and bookbinder's silk. I covered the existing pages with patterned paper, old book paper and music, fabric, acrylic paint, walnut ink, and Mod Podge. My altered book has a theme, so it is also somewhat of a **journal**. Art journals are **creative** springboards—the wild child of scrapbooking! So whether you choose a spiral bound journal or an out-of-date dictionary, the sky's the limit, and there's no telling where your creativity will take you!

— HEIDI

inspiration

creation

exploration

about the artists

DEBBIE CROUSE

Three years ago, I was scrapbooking in open-lab at Memory Lane when I noticed a "help wanted" sign. All day as I was working, I kept thinking, "The kids are older now, maybe I can do this. It could be fun." Little did I know what a change it would make in my life. Soon after I was hired, I met Robin Johnson, who was teaching classes at ML. I loved her from the first time we met, and she is one of the nicest people you will ever meet. She asked me to help her with some samples for a trade show to debut her line of vellum. Soon after, *Designing with Vellum* was in the works, and Robin asked if I would do some non-scrapbooking items to be included in the book. What fun that was!

Meanwhile, I was still working at ML and a cute blonde somehow left her scrapbook in the store. We noticed how amazing the scrapbooking was and called her to pick it up. Meet Heidi Swapp. She entered like a whirlwind and things have never been quite the same since. She is such a dynamo and can outrun us all (literally)! Robin brought the three of us together for the book *Designing with Notions*. We thought we made a pretty well-rounded team, touching on different styles and techniques.

During this time, we became acquainted with Julie Turner, who had started teaching at ML. She is wonderful, so thoughtful, and has a way of making you feel like you are the most important person around. Known for her classic style, Julie joined the group for a new venture, *Designing with Textures*. What a fun, tiring, and exciting adventure this has been. How lucky I am to have crossed paths with these ladies. They are truly talented and inspiring and are my treasured friends.

I have been married to my wonderful husband Skip for 27 years. We have four children: Jared, Emali, Skyler, and Logan. My son, Jared, and his wife, Kathy, have two handsome sons, Cole and Will, whom we all adore. Yes, that would make me the grandma of the group, but I've decided that is a good thing. When I'm not creating projects, I love to shop, watch my kids' sporting events, take pictures, and spend time with family and friends.

ROBIN JOHNSON

My husband Andrew and I just celebrated our 15th wedding anniversary. It's hard to believe we've been married that long. I am so grateful I have been a scrapbooker for 10 of those years! The memories of our life together will live on through our scrapbooks. We have been blessed with four children: Crissy, Lizzie, Sarah, and Devin. Their lives inspire me to create. I enjoy being with my family, spending time with friends, teaching, traveling, playing the piano, and, of course, scrapbooking.

HEIDI SWAPP

I live in Mesa, Arizona, with my husband Eric and our three kids, Colton, Cory, and Quincy. They keep me on my toes and give me a lot to laugh at and photograph! I would never have imagined that scrapbooking would become such a big part of my life, but I love it! I enjoy teaching at a local scrapbook store because it pushes me to come up with new material and allows me to interact with so many creative and wonderful people. In addition to scrapbooking, I love to travel, bike, stay up late, talk on the phone, and take pictures.

JULIE TURNER

My greatest joy is spending time with my three children, John, Jackson, and Jillian as their mom and as their homeschool teacher. That's how I discovered my love of scrapbooking. I started chronicling our school activities, and now scrapbooking has become a way to remember all the happy moments of raising a family and the 20 years of marriage to my terrific husband, Joel. My children already like to look at the albums, and I believe their great-grandchildren will enjoy the books just as much. Our family lives in Gilbert, Arizona.

& author

ERIN TRIMBLE

I grew up in Glendale, Arizona, and I married my high school sweetheart, Brian. We now live in Surprise with our daughter, Eliza. Brian and I love watching her play and learn. I earned my degree in secondary education from Arizona State University, and I went on to earn a Master's degree from Northern Arizona University.

A former high school English teacher, I now stay home with Eliza and teach an English class at Glendale Community College. In my free time, I enjoy making cards, writing and receiving letters, shopping, and doing primitive stitcheries.

about us

Autumn Leaves began in the stationery industry six years ago. At one point, they noticed that the sales of their paper were going up, but the sales of their envelopes were going down. After some research, they discovered that the paper was being purchased by scrapbookers who, of course, didn't need the envelope! They recognized the perfect match between their beautiful papers and the scrapbookers desire to create beautiful pages. A new company was born!

Autumn Leaves began producing stickers and vellum pages - some of the most artistic and beautiful vellum on the market. They also acquired Whispers, which is a vellum line. They decided to begin publishing idea books and realized the need for an idea book all about vellum. In September of 2001, they published *Designing with Vellum* by Robin Johnson. The success was amazing and it is now in its third printing.

Designing With Notions is the second book in the "The Sophisticated Scrapbook Series." And this book, *Designing With textures* is the third. In "Textures," wonderfully innovative designer Heidi Swapp heads a team of master scrapbookers as they search out some of the most unique and beautiful surfaces to ever find their way into your memories.

Autumn Leaves plans to continue with papers, vellums, stickers and books. Watch for new product releases throughout the year as the line grows and their forward thinking continues.

Jeff Lam is the owner and creative director for Autumn Leaves.

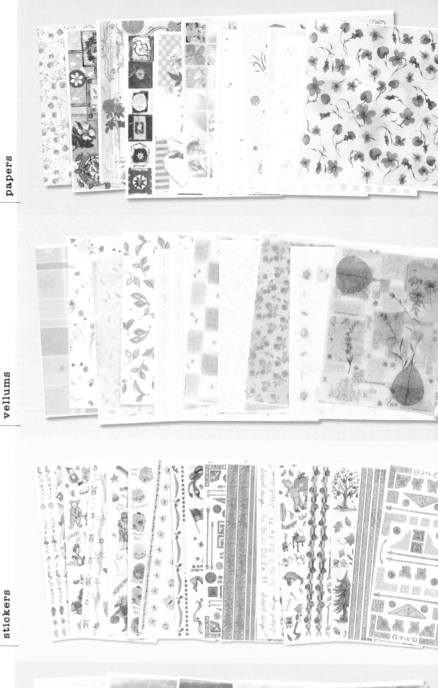

papers

vellums

stickers

whispers

Autumn Leaves
For Scrapbooking

...continued

books

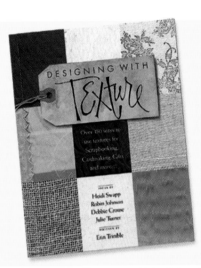

solid colored vellums

card stock

autumn leaves

4917 Genesta Ave.
Encino, CA 91316

1.800.588.6707 or 1.818.784.2731
1.800.380.6776 (fax)

For information, contact:

Josie Kinnear [OPERATIONS MANAGER]
Alanna Arthur [PROJECTS MANAGER]
Tim Collins [MARKETING DIRECTOR]

For all your card stock needs,
and the largest selection of
colored vellums in scrapbooking,
ask your retailer to carry the
National Card Stock line,
a division of Autumn Leaves.